Days of our Lives

50 Years

Greg Meng

Published by Sourcebooks, Inc.
P.O. Box 4410, Naperville, Illinois 60567-4410
(630) 961-2168
www.sourcebooks.com

Library of Congress Cataloging-in-Publication Data is on file with the publisher.

Printed and bound in the United States of America.
WOZ 10 9 8 7 6 5 4 3

"*Days of our Lives* hasn't just been in our homes for 50 years. It's also in our DNA, packing a power and punch that is incomparable in the daytime drama landscape. This beloved show is famous for its epic twists and crazy turns: Premature burial! Biblical plagues! Demonic possession! But this is not what keeps us loyally devoted and coming back, year in, year out. We return for the love—love of romance, love of friendship, love of family. When we make our daily trip to sleepy little Salem to visit with the Brady and Horton and Kiriakis clans, and even those impossible, badass DiMeras, we feel a marvelous sense of bliss and comfort and connection. This show is so much more than entertainment. It makes us feel like we've come home."

— Michael Logan, *TV Guide Magazine*

This book is dedicated

with appreciation
to NBC, the place we've called home for 50 years,
to our partner Sony, who keeps us safely in Salem

with gratitude
to the cast, writers, staff, and crew, who breathe the life into Salem,
to Ken Corday, who brings the heart and soul to Salem

with love
to our family of fans who inspire us,
… keeping the sands flowing through the hourglass.

"Launched during the Johnson administration, *Days of our Lives* was quite literally the first to inject bubbles into what we have come to know and love as daytime soaps—it's signature hourglass as ubiquitous to American pop culture as VW Beetles and the Frisbee. Its engrossing tales of love and marriage not only entertain but boldly and impressively endure—and will continue to survive the sands of time!"

— Lynette Rice, TV Editor At Large, *Entertainment Weekly*

Table of Contents

"One thing about daytime, there are colorful people in daytime. You are never bored."

— Pat Falken Smith, former Head Writer, *Days of our Lives*

BROUGHT TO YOU IN LIVING COLOR

Days of our Lives, the original daytime drama broadcast in color, premiered on NBC November 8, 1965.

LOCATION, LOCATION, LOCATION

As the first soap opera to be set in the rural Midwest, the show takes place in the town of Salem, USA—which is home to the characters and families millions of fans have grown to love, hate, love-to-hate, and admire.

AGELESS AND ENDURING

The longest running scripted series on NBC, *Days of our Lives* is grounded on the strong, Midwestern family values of Tom and Alice Horton and their children. These beliefs endure the test of time even as they are constantly challenged by other families, such as the powerful DiMeras—a family run by ruthless patriarch Stefano. With characters whom we love to root for and story lines that evolve with the times, *Days of our Lives* has proven to be lasting and eternal as it is shared from generation to generation.

COLORFUL

Possessed by the Devil!... In love with my brother?... Back from the dead!... Young love... Buried alive!... Love triangles... I now pronounce you husband and husband... Buckle up. It's quite a ride! There is always something happening in Salem.

FAMILY

As a longtime member of the Corday Productions family, it is a privilege to present this memory book: a collection of rare photos providing a big picture view while reflecting the heart and soul of the show through some of the beloved and iconic stories during the first 50 years. As eldest Horton granddaughter Julie reminisces with us about some of these unforgettable moments, we experience part of their lives... as they grow into responsible adults, encounter overwhelming challenges, fall in love, have children, and suffer the loss of loved ones.... the circle of life in our town... Salem, USA.

Greg Meng
Co-Executive Producer,
Executive In Charge Of Production
Days of our Lives

In Salem, USA, it's all about family. Brothers fighting over the same woman. Mothers meddling in their children's love lives. Grandmothers stealing buses to help their granddaughters escape the bad guys. (Okay, maybe that's just one awesome grandmother in particular.) It's these interactions between generations of each family that provide the heart and backbone of *Days of our Lives*.

Over the past 50 years, a myriad of different clans have called Salem "home," and whether it's the heroic Hortons or the dastardly DiMeras, each family has its own distinct persona.

The Good…

The Hortons	Tom and Alice headed up this loving, close-knit, upper middle class family. Though traditional, the Hortons have always evolved with the times.
The Bradys	Salt-of-the-earth and true-blue, the working-class Bradys are full of Irish spirit and moxie.
The Carvers	Well-respected, devoted, and kind, the Carvers are leaders of the community.
The Hernandezes	The Hernandez clan, having come from the wrong side of the tracks, has been on both sides of the law. However, the siblings are all good-hearted and fiercely loyal to each other.
The Johnsons	The Johnson siblings may not have grown up together, but once they were reunited as adults, they became very close. Their difficult, abusive childhood has made each of them strong.
The Jonases	The Jonases didn't learn of their familial connections until later in life. However, they are now making up for lost time and learning what it means to be a family.

The Bad…

The DiMeras	Devious, unscrupulous, and at many times, diabolical, the wealthy DiMeras tend to be larger than life villains (with a few notable exceptions, of course).

The Not-So-Bad… Not-So-Good

The Kiriakises	This Greek dynasty is a mixed bag. Patriarch Victor is known to dabble in criminal activities, while his descendants and other relatives sometimes have ethical lapses but are generally decent people.
Kate's Brood	Kate Roberts can be ruthless and cunning but her children tend to be a little more kindhearted.
The Deverauxes	This political newspaper family was once led by Harper, who turned out to be a serial killer. Meanwhile, Jack and his children have made terrible mistakes but managed to turn their lives around.

"Hope and Stefano come from opposite ends of the spectrum—one darkness, one light… but the thing they have in common is their passion to defend and preserve their families."

— Kristian Alfonso, "Hope Brady," *Days of our Lives*

Family

"The one key word to describe *Days of our Lives*… 'family.'"

— Ken Corday

Hello. My name is Julie Olson Banning Anderson Williams. This is my favorite photo of my grandparents, Tom and Alice Horton, sitting in their living room which has been—and continues to be—the central gathering place for our family.

I can't say I made life easy for my darling grandparents. As a teenager, I was constantly rebelling. On November 8, 1965, I was even arrested for shoplifting a mink stole from Bartlett's department store! Soon after, I moved in with Grandpa and Grandma, and they did their best to set me on the straight and narrow. Without their love and guidance, I know I wouldn't be the woman I am today.

Over the course of five decades, I've pretty much been through it all. I've laughed and cried, suffered unspeakable loss and celebrated incredible triumphs, but most of all, I've come to love and respect my family with all my heart. I have so many special memories of my time in Salem. In particular, I will always fondly remember baking donuts with my grandmother, Alice, singing and dancing with my beloved husband, Doug, and giving birth to my son, David—all part of the great circle of life.

I am so proud to be part of the memories in this book and the stories we will continue to share… of the families of Salem. After all, we do know that whatever the future holds for us, with the strength of family, love will conquer all.

Julie

"Tom and Alice Horton represent a core of stability—to reflect, not generate story."
— Bill Bell, former Head Writer, *Days of our Lives*

The Good...

THE HORTONS—SALEM'S FIRST FAMILY

The first family of Salem is the Hortons. This family has seen more than their fair share of drama, romance, and conflict over 50 years. The Hortons have always been the moral compass of Salem with their rich, deep, traditional family values.

When *Days of our Lives* premiered in 1965, Alice was going through "empty nest" syndrome as all of her children were grown and living their own lives. Dr. Tom Horton was everyone's favorite doctor in town, a trusted confidante, and a loving and supportive father. A match made in heaven, their enduring love story was an inspiration to the other couples in Salem.

Tom Horton and Alice Grayson Horton:

Children	Grandchildren	Great-grandchildren
Tommy	Julie	David
Addie	Steven	Spencer
Mickey	Sandy	Jeremy
Bill	Mike	Nick
Marie	Jessica	Nathan
	Melissa	Shawn-Douglas
	Hope	Zack
	Jennifer	Ciara
	Lucas	Abigail
	Sarah	JJ
		Will
		Allie

Great-great-grandchildren

Scotty
Claire
Arianna

Addie, Alice, Marie, Mickey, Tom, Bill, and Tom Jr.

Opposite top photo: Mickey, Tom Jr., Bill, and Tom

Opposite bottom photo: Julie, Laura, Susan Martin, Sandy, Alice, and Marie with Tom

162

DR. MARK BROOKS

DR. WM. HORTON

HORTON DOCTORS

Tom Horton, following in his father's footsteps, was a well-respected doctor. He eventually became Chief of Staff at Salem University Hospital.

Tom pushed his oldest son, Tommy Jr., to also become a physician. Tommy's medical career was put on hold when he took off to fight in the Korean War—where he supposedly died. However, when Dr. Mark Brooks came to Salem, Tom soon realized "Mark" was actually Tommy, who now had amnesia and was unrecognizable due to plastic surgery to repair damage to his face.

Tom's youngest son, Bill, was also a beloved doctor and his wife, Laura, was a successful psychiatrist. Tom's youngest daughter, Marie, started out as a lab technician, then later became a nurse.

As the Horton family continued to grow, so did the number of those who emulated Tom by becoming doctors and nurses.

Grandchildren Sandy and Mike became doctors, while Jessica enrolled in nursing school.

Great-grandchild Nathan was also a physician. Nick had a stint as a lab tech like his grandmother, Marie.

Great-great-grandchild Scotty Banning left Salem in order to attend medical school.

The Good...

THE BRADYS

The blue-collar Bradys are the salt-of-the-earth clan of Salem, who run a family business, a staple of Salem, called Brady's Pub. They are a tight-knit and loyal group, who stick together through thick and thin, through unbelievable heartbreak and tragedies. While they were always in town, the Bradys weren't seen on-screen until the 1980s when audiences were first introduced to tough cop Roman Brady, and the rest of the family of characters soon followed. Roman's mother Caroline and his father, a former longshoreman, the late Shawn Brady, owned the Pub.

Shawn Brady and Caroline:

Children	Grandchildren		Great-grandchildren
Roman	Carrie	Stephanie	Will
Kimberly	Eric	Joey	Johnny
Kayla	Sami	Shawn-Douglas	Allie
Bo	Rex	Chelsea	Sydney
Frankie	Cassie	Zack	Claire
Max	Andrew	Ciara	Carrie's child with
	Jeannie		Austin
	(Theresa)		

Great-great-grandchildren

Arianna

The Bradys are a perfect example of how love—not blood—ties a family together as not only are Frankie and Max adopted, but also Bo is actually the love child of Caroline and Victor. The Bradys have been regularly challenged with a series of cataclysmic events—Roman was believed dead for years, Kayla was once deaf, Kimberly was temporarily blinded, and Bo was devastated to learn that Victor—not Shawn—was his biological pop.

BRADY'S PUB CLAM CHOWDER RECIPE
Total Time: 50min
Prep: 25 min
Cook: 25 min
Serves: 4

Ingredients:

4 dozen clams
½ cup minced onion
1 cup flour
½ cup celery
½ cup diced carrots

1 ½ cups cubed potatoes
3 thick slices of bacon, cut up
¾ cup butter
1 quart half and half cream
2 tsp salt & pepper

Directions:

1. Add 2 cups of water to a large pot and boil clams for 8 minutes, or until all clams have opened. Strain the liquid from the pot through a mesh strainer and reserve.

2. Chop up the clams and add a few drops of olive oil To the pot. Bring the pot to medium heat and toss in the bacon.

3. When the bacon crisps, combine onions, celery, carrots, potatoes, gradually sprinkling the flour while mixing.

4. Pour in the reserved clam juice, butter, half and half cream, salt and pepper. Bring to a boil and reduce to a simmer for 10 to 15 minutes.

BRADY'S PUB

Brady's Pub quickly became the hot spot for the town of Salem, whether you wanted to grab cup of coffee, a stiff drink, have a chitchat, or a hearty meal and a bowl of their famous clam chowder.

Caroline continues at the helm where she lends a supportive ear to troubled friends and relatives.

The Bad…

THE DIMERAS

"… As the phoenix rises from the ashes…"

The DiMeras are extremely wealthy but morally bankrupt. Stefano is the head of this nefarious clan, which consists of offspring from a variety of different mothers. With each child, Stefano has proven over and over he is willing to do anything to secure their happiness—even at the expense of outsiders. However, Stefano's love often comes with a heavy price. He is controlling and manipulative, and many of his children learn too late they must avoid succumbing to his evil influence. Sadly, most of Stefano's kin have met untimely demises, whereas Stefano always manages to escape death and "rise from the ashes." Hence, his nickname, "The Phoenix."

Bio-sons	Bio-daughters	Adopted	Grandchildren
Andre	Renée	Tony	Theo
Benjy	Megan	Kristen	Steven
EJ	Lexie	Peter	Johnny
Chad			Sydney
			Grace

Stefano's feud with the Bradys has spanned more than four decades. Roman was his initial target, which then led to his obsession with Roman's wife, Marlena. Many of Stefano's most outrageous plots have centered around his desire to win the affections of his "Queen of the Night." Stefano's other longtime adversary is John Black, the man he brainwashed and used as his "Pawn" for many years. Despite all his criminal activities, the Salem PD has never been able to keep DiMera behind bars for very long—and he continues to wreak havoc to this very day.

Pictured below: Andre, EJ, and Chad.

                    VICTOR
        I found out a lot about Stefano
        DiMera's parents.

                     BO

        I've never thought of him as having

        parents. That makes him seem human.

Above: Kristen and Stefano

Opposite page: top left, clockwise, Benjy, Peter, Stefano and Renée, and Megan

Lexie's Turn to the Dark Side

Lexie Carver received the shock of her life when she learned crime lord Stefano DiMera was her biological father! Though Lexie had always been a kind and compassionate doctor, she eventually succumbed to her father's wicked influence and started down a path of self-destruction.

Abe and Lexie had long wanted children but had trouble conceiving. In 2000, they decided to adopt instead. Stefano, who mistakenly believed Hope was carrying his child, saw the perfect opportunity to help his newfound daughter—and himself. He convinced Lexie and Abe to adopt the baby of Dr. Rolf's niece, Marlo. However, Stefano wanted "his" child to be raised within the family—so he switched Marlo's baby with Hope's once the two boys were born. Once Lexie learned the truth, she went to great lengths to keep Issac—even though it meant keeping her good friend Hope from her own son.

Lexie's Rap Sheet

- During an argument with her uncle Rolf, Marlo fell down the stairs and broke her neck. Lexie was horrified when she found Marlo's dead body at her father's house, but Stefano vaguely warned her if she told Abe the truth, she'd be jeopardizing her future with Issac. Lexie kept quiet and even went so far as to misdirect Abe's police investigation so he wouldn't figure out a newly-discovered, unidentified body was actually Marlo.

- Lexie panicked when Marlo's ex, Glen Reiber, came to Salem, claiming Issac was his son. Glen demanded a paternity test, and Stefano, knowing Hope was raising Glen's baby, assured Lexie all would work out. However, Lexie secretly asked Brandon Walker to switch the paternity test, and Brandon used a swab from Hope's child, J.T. When Brandon informed Lexie the test came back positive, she was completely stunned—this meant Hope was raising Marlo and Glen's baby, and Lexie was raising Hope's! Lexie and Brandon kept this a secret from Abe.

- Stefano covered up the results of the DNA test, and Lexie and Abe moved into the DiMera mansion. When Hope, Bo, and John all started becoming suspicious of Lexie, she realized she needed to distract them. So Lexie donned a fabulous red dress and threw a "Mother of the Year" party for Hope—allowing Rolf the chance to try turning Hope back into Princess Gina. The plan failed.

- Glen's wife, Barb, figured out the baby switch and tried to blackmail Lexie. Lexie balked, and Barb blabbed the truth about the two babies. Lexie lied to Abe, pretending she only recently found out what happened.

- Glen and Barb got custody of J.T., and Bo and Hope sued for custody of Issac. Lexie leaked information about the Bradys to the newspaper, making them look like unfit parents.

- Lexie urged Abe to help her fight to keep Issac, but even though it broke his heart, Abe knew they had to return the baby to his rightful parents. Lexie refused to give up the child she so desperately loved and decided to flee the country with Issac. However, she was caught and arrested.

Bo and Hope reunited with their son and renamed him Zack. Meanwhile, Lexie lashed out at Abe for not taking her side. She and Abe continued to be estranged for quite some time—and while they were apart, Lexie slept with Brandon. Lexie ended up pregnant, but the child turned out to be Abe's. Over time, Lexie managed to redeem herself, and the two eventually reconciled, happily raising their new son, Theo, together as a family.

THE KIRIAKISES

Powerful, wealthy, and ruthless, with an undying allegiance to the family unit best describes the Kiriakis family. The patriarch, Victor Kiriakis, will do whatever it takes at any cost to protect those he loves, and to bring down his enemies. Victor arrived on the Salem scene in 1985 with ties to a drug and prostitution ring. He is the founder of Titan Industries, which continues to be one of the major corporate businesses in Salem and the center of much boardroom intrigue. Victor is extremely protective of his family, and will go to great lengths to do what he thinks is best for them.

Children	**Grandchildren**
Bo	Brady
Isabella	Shawn-Douglas
Philip	Chelsea
	Zack
	Tyler
	Ciara

Great-grandchildren	**Nephews**
Claire	Justin
	Xander
	Sonny (grandnephew)

Victor has been quite the ladies' man throughout his time in Salem, having married: Nicole, Carly, Vivian, Kate (although that was later proved invalid), and his current wife, Maggie. However, there will always be a special place in his heart for Caroline Brady, the mother of his son, Bo.

Attorney Justin Kiriakis is Victor's nephew. Justin and Adrienne's son, Sonny Kiriakis, currently resides in Salem and continues the family legacy.

Victor with ex-wives: Kate, Vivian, Nicole, and Carly

Justin and Victor in Greece

Philip and Victor

Isabella

Sonny, Adrienne, and Justin

THE WEDDING OF MAGGIE HORTON AND VICTOR KIRIAKIS

Never underestimate what the love of a good woman can do for a man. Victor Kiriakis hadn't had much luck in the marriage department and Maggie was a widow, still mourning the loss of her beloved Mickey, when a spark started to develop between the powerful Greek crime lord and the former farm girl.

Friendship blossomed into love and Victor and Maggie set a wedding date, November 8, 2011. A snowstorm threatened to mar Maggie and Victor's celebration, but some guests, including Maggie's son Daniel and granddaughter Melanie, were able to brave the elements and be there. Victor offered to postpone the wedding if she wanted, but Maggie didn't want any more time to pass. Melanie felt that as long as Maggie and Victor were together then that's all that mattered.

Daniel was still adjusting to the news that Maggie was his mother, the result of some stolen eggs. He maintained that he wanted nothing more than to see her happy and agreed to her request that he give her away. Maggie and Victor were married by Justin, Victor's nephew, in an intimate, informal, but lovely ceremony.

"Happily ever after" isn't a road that's often traveled in Salem, but Victor and Maggie have made a go of it.

Salem Tradition

In Salem, you can always count on certain things—Stefano coming back from the dead… Bo referring to Hope as "Fancy Face"… Sami plotting, then getting married, then plotting again. However, there are some traditions that rise above all others, that make the town of Salem wonderfully unique and a special place to live. These traditions warm the heart, feed the soul, and bring families together in times of great joy and sorrow. Salem just wouldn't be Salem without the following:

The Horton Christmas Ornaments

Every Christmas, the Horton family gathers in Tom and Alice's living room and decorates the tree with handmade ornaments featuring the names of every member of the Horton clan. The original ornaments were made by Tom's mother, and as the family grew, new ones were added to the tree. With as many children, grandchildren, great-grandchildren—and even great-great-grandchildren—as Tom and Alice have, it's impossible for everyone to make it home for Christmas each year. But these ornaments serve as a reminder of their loved ones who are either scattered across the globe or who have passed on. No matter where their family may be, it's a way of bringing everyone together.

The Reading of the Christmas Story at University Hospital

Being stuck in a hospital during the holidays is never any fun, especially for kids. On Christmas Day, the staff at University Hospital puts on a festive celebration for the sick children. "Santa" comes bearing gifts, then one special Salem resident settles in to read the Christmas Story from the Bible. It's a high honor to be chosen, and past luminaries include Tom Horton, Alice Horton, Doug Williams, Roman Brady, Jennifer Horton, Steve Johnson, Chloe Lane, and Abigail Deveraux.

Alice's Donuts

Alice Horton's donuts are legendary, not only for their "yum" factor but also for their ability to make her family and friends feel loved. Whenever Alice would invite someone to bake these delectable treats with her, she used the opportunity to bond with that person and offer sage advice when needed. Before passing away in 2010, Alice handed down the secret recipe to Jennifer to make sure the tradition continued. Of course, while the donuts are still a Horton family favorite, it's not quite the same without Alice's loving touch.

Patriotic Celebrations

Salem is a town that likes to show off its red, white, and blue. For many years, the Hortons and Bradys often got together for a lively Independence Day BBQ. In more recent years, a Fourth of July picnic by the lake has become popular for everyone!

"Apparently if you get your name on a Christmas ornament, you're in for life!"

— Jack Deveraux

Christmas in Salem also brings another holiday tradition. Starting in 1983, Santa visits sick children in the hospital and a prominent citizen of Salem will read the Christmas story to them. Some who have read the story are Dr. Tom Horton (shown above), Alice Horton, Roman Brady, Bo Brady, Jennifer Deveraux, Steven "Patch" Johnson, Doug Williams, and Chloe Lane.

"They may be scattered all over the world, but once this time of year, they're all right here in our living room and we're all together."

— Alice Horton, reflecting on family while admiring the tree full of ornaments in 1992

"Every Christmas we do this, to remind us of what's important in life. To remember what it's really about—family, friends, and love. And as we hang each of the ornaments, let's think about that person and hold a special thought for them…"

— Tom Horton, right before the hanging of the Horton ornaments in 1991

"Whenever I got out of line, you made me bake donuts with you. I didn't realize it then, but we were really making memories. You've given me so many—all of us. You are the heart of this family, Gram."

— Jennifer Horton to her grandmother, Alice Horton

"For every empty heart, there is a perfect recipe to fill it up."

— Alice Horton

ALICE'S FAMOUS CAKE DONUTS

Hint: *Only attempt to make the donuts when your heart is filled with love.*

Ingredients:

2 eggs

1 cup of sugar

1 cup of milk

5 tablespoons melted shortening

1 teaspoon vanilla extract

4 cups all-purpose flour, sifted before measuring

4 teaspoons baking powder

½ teaspoon salt

1 stick butter, melted

6 cups of love

In a large bowl, beat the eggs until foamy. Gradually add the sugar.

Beating constantly, stir in the milk, shortening, and vanilla.

Sift together the flour, baking powder, and salt. Add to the dry ingredients, mixing well. Cover and chill the dough for 30 minutes to 1 hour for easier handling.

Preheat the oven to 450 degrees. Spray a baking sheet with vegetable cooking spray.

Roll out or pat the dough on a lightly floured board to a ½ inch thickness. Cut with a donut cutter. Place the donuts and holes on the baking sheet, about 1 inch apart. Bake for 10 to 15 minutes or until golden brown.

Brush each donut and donut holes with melted butter and roll in Cinnamon Sugar to coat all sides.

Makes about 36 donuts.

Cinnamon Sugar Topping:

1 cup of sugar

1 teaspoon of cinnamon

In a small bowl, combine the sugar and cinnamon, blending well.

"Baked with love" were Grandma Alice's donuts. She would spend hours in the kitchen making these delectables, which became a staple and a must-have tradition all over town. Those lucky enough to sample the donuts are in for a real treat! When Alice passed, Jennifer, Hope, and I all continued this baking tradition, but everyone agrees there is no topping Grandma's recipe for living: follow your heart, take care of the ones you love, and stay true to yourself… words of wisdom she would offer to those in need of an ear to listen, and some cheering up while serving them her fabulous donuts.

<u>EXCLUSIVE TO YOU IN YOUR AREA</u>

DOUBLE TIME -- "Days of Our Lives" doubles its airtime

as it goes from a half hour to a full hour <u>Monday,</u>

<u>April 21</u> (12:30-1:30 p.m. PT, in color). Series star

Macdonald Carey, who plays Dr. Tom Horton, and Susan

Seaforth Hayes (Julie) decide this calls for doubling the

size of the series' hourglass trademark.

(A)

SUSAN SEAFORTH HAYES (LEFT) AND MACDONALD CAREY

NBC-TV'S "DAYS OF OUR LIVES"

<u>MONDAY, APRIL 21, 1975</u>

3/18/75

YOUNG LOVE

Young love stories have been a hallmark of *Days of our Lives* since the show's inception. Here's a look back at some of the show's most memorable young star-crossed lovers!

David Martin and Julie Olson: Impulsive Julie actually heeded her grandfather Tom's advice and opted not to marry David but then he turned around and wed her best friend Susan.

Mike Horton and Trish Clayton: Nothing says "I love you" to your girlfriend like taking the fall for a crime she committed. That's just what Mike did after Trish snuffed her abusive step-dad.

David Banning and Valerie Grant: *Days of our Lives* touched on interracial romance with Julie's son, David, and Valerie, who was African-American, after David moved in with the Grant family.

Mike Horton and Margo Anderman: Mike and Margo's love story came to a sad end after she passed away from leukemia.

Bo Brady and Hope Williams: Bo and Hope's first shot at lovemaking was cut short by Hope's father Doug having a heart attack. The couple finally made love months later at Oak Alley in New Orleans.

Pete Jannings and Melissa Horton: Brash gang member Pete was captivated by Melissa, a soft-spoken angel, who always saw the good in Pete.

Frankie Brady and Jennifer Horton: High school sweethearts, Frankie and Jennifer eventually decided it was best if they remained pals.

Tanner Scofield and Molly Brinker: "Bad boy" and backwoods gal fell in love as they searched for their own moms.

Austin Reed and Carrie Brady: Carrie was on the way to making some bad choices, but she found a good guy in boxer Austin. They battled her sister and his brother to get to the altar.

Philip Kiriakis and Chloe Lane: Philip saw a different side to Chloe, cruelly nicknamed "Ghoul Girl," and fell in love.

Brady Black and Chloe Lane: Glammed up Chloe made beautiful music with fellow singer Brady.

Shawn Brady and Belle Black: Shawn's the son of Bo and Hope; Belle's the daughter of Marlena and John. They wed in 2007 and left Salem with their daughter Claire to see the world.

Will Horton and Sonny Kiriakis: Sonny helped Will through the struggle with his sexuality. Friendship turned to love and the two men were wed in 2014.

Eric Brady and Nicole Walker: Photographer Eric fell in love with aspiring model, Nicole. Her thirst for money and power drove them apart.

Young Love

HOPE'S 18TH BIRTHDAY PARTY

For Hope's 18th birthday, Doug threw a big, formal party for his "Princess" at Doug's Place. Hope was excited to bring Bo as her date and even gave him a tuxedo to wear to the event. Doug, on the other hand, was less than thrilled to have his daughter dating the young motorcycle-riding rebel. At the party, Bo and Hope shared a romantic dance as Liz sang, "Tonight, I Celebrate My Love." Things took a disastrous turn when the couple privately exchanged gifts. Bo gave Hope a book of poems given to him by Shawn, while Hope presented him with an expensive jacket. Bo bristled, feeling like she was trying to change him, and they ended up in a huge fight, causing Bo to storm off into the night. When Bo arrived back at his place, he found Hope waiting for him. As he vented his frustrations, he couldn't help but blurt out that he loved her! He pulled her into a passionate kiss, then they sank onto his bed, about to make love for the first time. However, they were soon interrupted by a pounding at the door—it was Doug! He ordered Hope to stay away from Bo, but she refused, insisting she was old enough to make her own decisions. Doug got so worked up, he ended up having a massive heart attack right on the spot! Thankfully, he survived. However, Hope was so guilt-ridden, she pulled away from Bo, putting a halt to their budding relationship.

On location at historic Oak Alley Plantation located on the Mississippi River in the community of Vacherie, Louisiana.

OAK ALLEY

While hiding out from Maxwell Hathaway, the adoptive father of Bo's obssessed former girlfriend, Megan, Bo, and Hope took refuge at an old Southern plantation house called Oak Alley. Soaking in the romantic atmosphere, Bo literally swept Hope off her feet and carried her up the grand staircase to the master bedroom, where they made love for the first time.

The next morning, Bo surprised Hope with a "marriage of the heart." The star-crossed lovers were able to block out the rest of the world and forget the dangers they were facing.

Dr. Marlena Evans Black
and
Mr. & Mrs. Beauregard Brady
request the honor of your
presence at the marriage of
their children,
Isabella Black
and
Shawn Douglas Brady
on Thanksgiving Day
at the Brady home.
A reception will follow
the ceremony at
the Brady Pub.

TANTALIZING TRIANGLES

Three's a crowd? You bet it is… especially when you're vying for the love of the same man or woman! Throughout five tumultuous decades of story lines on *Days of our Lives*, steamy and complex affairs of the heart have made for raw emotional drama, unbridled passion, and plenty of sneaky machinations and double-crossing. Just when you think your favorite character has a direct path to finally being with the one they love, think again! Someone will wind up pregnant, paralyzed, or dying, entrapping their partner into doing the right thing and staying married instead of allowing them to follow their heart. And don't count out someone returning from the dead, or from the past, to further mess up any chance of lovers' happiness. Some triangles can go on, and on, and on… keeping viewers on the edge of their seats.

These threesomes gave viewers plenty of angst, tears, and romance:

- Susan/David/Julie
- Addie/Doug/Julie
- Bill/Laura/Mickey
- Renée/Tony/Anna
- Carrie/Austin/Sami
- Roman/Marlena/John
- Hope/Bo/Billie
- Brady/Philip/Chloe
- Nicole/EJ/Sami
- Sonny/Will/Paul

Bo Brady, Steve Johnson, and Britta Englund shared a deep bond while abroad, even going so far as to get matching knife tattoos. Alas, the friendship ended horribly after Bo caught Britta and Steve in bed together. The two men had a knife fight during which Steve both lost an eye and gained a new nickname— "Patch."

"Three together, together forever!"

— Bo Brady, Steve Johnson, and Britta Englund's slogan

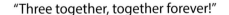

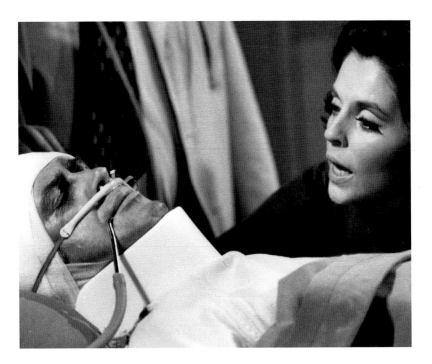

Julie/David/Susan

Julie was deeply saddened to learn that the man she loved, David Martin, had gotten her former friend Susan Hunter pregnant. The plan was for David and Susan to wed so that their child would be legitimate. But after David and Susan's son died while in his father's care, a distraught Susan killed David, forever closing the door on David and Julie's romance. However, a part of their love lived on—Julie was pregnant with David's son. Later, Mickey, Julie's uncle, defended Susan and she was acquitted on the grounds of temporary insanity.

Julie/Scott/Susan

Julie gave up her son with the late David Martin and later learned that he was being raised by widower Scott Banning. Upon learning that Susan was Scott's neighbor and nanny to his little boy, Julie sued for custody—and won! Scott wanted to be with his son so much that he agreed to marry Julie. In time, they both realized their union was a sham. Julie filed divorce papers, but once again fate intervened and Scott was killed, leaving Julie a widow.

Addie/Doug/Julie

Tired of losing men to Julie, Susan hired con man Brent Douglas (who changed his name to Doug Williams) to romance Julie away from Scott Banning. The plan took several twists: Doug and Julie ended up falling in love for real, but the couple quarreled one night which led to Doug's impulsive marriage to Addie, Julie's mother. Doug and Addie's relationship was solidified with the birth of their daughter Hope. Addie managed to survive leukemia, but perished after she was struck by a speeding automobile, saving little Hope's life in the process.

EXCLUSIVE TO YOU IN YOUR AREA

DREAM TRIANGLE -- In a disturbed dream fed by anxiety over her crumbling marriage, Patricia Barry, as Addie Williams (right) finds herself in a tug-of-war with her daughter Julie (Susan Seaforth) for possession of Addie's husband, Doug (Bill Hayes) on "Days of Our Lives" (Mondays through Fridays, 12:30-1 p.m., in color) over NBC-TV.

(L-R) SUSAN SEAFORTH, BILL HAYES, PATRICIA BARRY

NBC-TV'S "DAYS OF OUR LIVES"

MONDAYS THROUGH FRIDAYS   3/9/73

Sami/Austin/Carrie

Sami pursued Austin, her sister Carrie's boyfriend, with a relentless passion. Citing other unfaithful women in her family, Sami went after Austin, apologizing to no one. She got him to the altar by using "their" son Will as a pawn. But before the "I do's" could be exchanged Carrie announced that Lucas, not Austin, was Will's dad. Sami finally got her comeuppance courtesy of Carrie's left fist!

John/Marlena/Roman

Marlena returned to Salem after four years of captivity and soon learned that her husband "Roman" wasn't really Roman! The real Roman was freed from being Stefano's prisoner and reunited with his beloved "Doc," leaving John Black out in the cold. But John and Marlena couldn't deny their feelings. They had an affair, conceived a daughter (Belle), and, in time, made peace with Roman.

Bill/Laura/Mickey

One of the most popular and long-running triangles in *Days of our Lives* history was the tortured tale of two Horton brothers fighting over the same woman. Bill and Laura dated first, but it was Mickey who eventually walked down the aisle with the lovely psychiatrist. Bill never got over Laura, and one fateful night, he raped her in a drunken stupor. This led to Laura getting pregnant and giving birth to Mike. Everyone initially assumed the boy was Mickey's, including Bill who had no recollection of what he had done. Over the course of several years, the truth slowly came to light with Mickey being the last to know. In time, Mickey fell in love with Maggie, while Bill and Laura wed and had another child, Jennifer.

Kate/Victor/Vivian

Vivian Alamain used drugs and deception to get rid of Kate Roberts in order to become Victor Kiriakis' wife. Kate survived a plane crash and made her way back to Victor's home. The couple's happiness was short-lived, however, because Victor later had a stroke. He recovered but his relationship with Kate failed in the end not due to Viv, but because of their own foibles.

Philip/Chloe/Brady

Brady Black was more mature than brash Philip Kiriakis (even though Philip is technically Brady's uncle) and he soon won the heart of Philip's girlfriend Chloe. Brady's presence helped her get through a battle with leukemia. Later, Chloe let Brady think she was dead after being horribly scarred. She recovered, wed Brady, and the honeymooners left town.

Abe/Lexie/Tek

Lexie betrayed her marriage to Abe by falling for ex-ISA agent Thomas Edward Kramer aka "Tek." Abe discovered the two having sex in a motel room and blasted his wife with the harshest words he could muster up: "You really are a DiMera after all!" In time, Tek left Salem and the Carvers reunited, in part, for the sake of their son Theo.

Austin/Carrie/Mike

Carrie grew close to her good friend Mike while she supported him through a groundless sexual harassment lawsuit. The good doctor fell in love with Carrie, who was feeling distanced from her husband Austin. Carrie and Mike had an affair. When Austin found out, he decked him. Carrie and Austin split; Mike and Carrie moved to Israel so he could be near his son Jeremy. Carrie returned to Salem years later, revealing that her relationship with Mike was over.

Carly/Hope/Bo

When Bo thought Hope was dead, he turned to Dr. Carly Manning for support. They fell in love and were to be married, only Carly's near-death experience from being buried alive and the revelation that she had a long lost son caused her to leave Salem and Bo behind. Over fifteen years later, she returned to Salem and reunited with Bo, who was estranged from Hope. Soon, Carly realized that Bo didn't love anyone the way he loved Hope.

Nicole/EJ/Sami

What made Nicole's fascination with EJ so compelling is that she understood him better than most women do—and she still wanted him anyway. Nicole, after miscarrying EJ's baby, kidnapped Sami's daughter so she could raise EJ's child. The plan failed. EJ and Sami married, only to have their happiness cut short by his untimely "death."

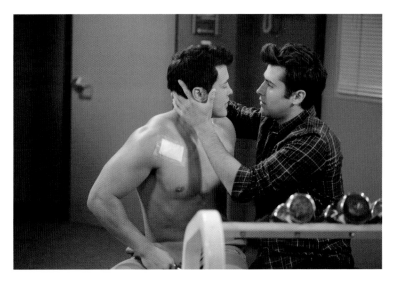

Will/Paul/Sonny

Sonny and Will overcame many hurdles to get to the altar including Will going through the "coming out" process. Alas, the honeymoon was over when Will compromised not only his journalistic ethics, but also his marriage vows by sleeping with interview subject Paul Narita, a closeted professional baseball player. Sonny and Paul were once lovers, further complicating matters.

RENÉE/TONY/ANNA

Renée DuMonde was jealous of Anna who was married to Tony and carrying his child. Renée made a small hole in the side of Anna's boat, hoping it would sink and Anna would drown. However, Tony came back early from a trip and accompanied his wife on the boat which soon began to sink. Tony was knocked unconscious and Anna rescued him. However, she lost their baby as a result.

DAYS OF OUR LIVES CELEBRATES 50 YEARS OF SUPERCOUPLES!—Michael Maloney

All soaps have showcased couples falling in love, but the storytelling, chemistry among actors, and a special magic have all contributed to put *Days of our Lives* into a league of its own when it comes to supercouples. Audiences become invested in a couple when they see each person in it learning from the other and also making thoughtful gestures. "Romance is doing things for the other person that's going to make them happy," says Sheri Anderson, former Head Writer of *Days of our Lives*, who has penned tales for many of your favorite couples. "People are looking for honesty. They're looking to see that relationships can work and how they can apply that to their own lives."

Some of the most successful pairings on *Days of our Lives* have come from characters who aren't in the same social class as the person to whom they're attracted. "You can't be on the same level because then you're not having to adjust," Anderson notes.

The beauty of couples on *Days of our Lives* is that they're all supercouples to so many devotees of the show. "We'd hear from fans that John and Marlena or Roman and Marlena or Bo and Hope or Patch and Kayla were their favorites but they also feel strongly about Pete and Melissa and Neil and Liz. I've heard people say that their favorite couple is Mickey and Maggie! Personally, I have about four or five that are my favorites including Tony and Anna because of their sophistication," Anderson says. "I truly enjoyed writing for all of them."

Here are the top supercouples from *Days of our Lives'* first 50 years:

- **Doug Williams and Julie Olson:** They endured Doug's marriage to Julie's mother, Julie being scarred in a fire, Doug's ill-advised union with Lee Dumonde and a host of other obstacles on the road to happiness.

- **Bo Brady and Hope Williams:** Bo bursting into Hope's bridal room before her planned marriage to Larry Welch and taking her away on a "borrowed" cop's motorcycle remains, arguably, the most memorable moment in the duo's history.

- **Roman Brady and Marlena Evans:** He showed up on her doorstep with a sleeping bag, determined to protect her from the Salem Strangler. Along the way, they fell in love, becoming one of Salem's most beloved and popular pairs.

- **John Black and Marlena Evans:** It started off with Marlena believing that John was Roman brought back to life. In time, the duo developed their own special love that continues to endure.

- **Steve "Patch" Johnson and Kayla Brady:** A classic bad boy/good girl romance, Kayla's heart melts each and every time Patch calls her "sweetness"— and so do the viewers.

- **Shane Donovan and Kimberly Brady:** The dashing spy swooped in to rescue the young woman who'd been sexually abused by her uncle. Later, she'd help save him from a crime lord.

- **Jack Deveraux and Jennifer Horton:** She's the good girl who grounded the former bad boy. Along the way, they shared a lot of laughs.

- **Justin Kiriakis and Adrienne Johnson:** Justin was a playboy who changed his ways to help abused Adrienne, who became even stronger thanks to Justin's love.

- **Carrie Brady and Austin Reed:** Not even her scheming sister Sami could keep beautiful Carrie from having her happily ever after with the dashing Austin.

- **Tony DiMera and Anna Fredericks:** These two were as witty and charming as they were sophisticated!

- **Neil Curtis and Liz Chandler:** Her ties to the DiMera clan kept them apart, but viewers knew that Liz always had Neil on her mind.

"There are couples who are hot, and there are supercouples… those couples who have some kind of chemistry. It's a combination of love, attraction, romance, fantasy—all those elements."

— Andrea Payne, Editor at *Soap Opera Digest* in 1984

THE WEDDING OF MARLENA EVANS AND "ROMAN BRADY" (JOHN BLACK)

Marlena believed a miracle had happened when her beloved Roman came back to her after he had been "killed" by Stefano. While Roman was indeed alive, it was actually a man named John Black who returned to Salem, believing he was Shawn and Caroline's firstborn. Wanting to reaffirm their commitment, Marlena and "Roman" renewed their 1983 wedding vows in front of their family and friends.

Tamara (Marilyn McCoo), Marlena's pal, sang the couple's love song "Up Where We Belong" as part of the 1986 ceremony. The bride and groom took turns reading passages from the following poem written by Johann Wolfgang von Goethe as part of their ceremony:

"That is the true season of love, when we believe that we alone can love, that no one could ever have loved so before us, and that no one will love in the same way as us."

"It was 17 months, 3 weeks, and 2 days, that's how long I hurt," Marlena said, commenting on how much time had passed between Roman's "death" and their vow renewal. "That's how long my heart ached to be with you."

It turned out to be five years before the real Roman returned. He and Marlena tried to make a go of it, but, in time, Marlena and John reunited after they realized their love was not to be denied.

DOUG

(Love) beareth all things, believeth all things, hopeth all things, endureth all things,... (1st Corinthians 13:7)

Julie

Love never faileth.

THE WEDDING OF JULIE OLSON AND DOUG WILLIAMS

In 1976, before Doug and Julie were to marry, Doug's ex-wife Kim Douglas returned claiming she and Doug had never legally divorced. After months of trying to win Doug back, Kim confessed that they had been divorced legally for many years. Shortly after, Julie and Doug finally got married. This was a very special date for eager fans thrilled about the chance to watch these star-crossed lovers finally get hitched.

THE WEDDING OF KIMBERLY BRADY AND SHANE DONOVAN

Shane Donovan surprised his then fiancée Kimberly Brady with an impromptu ceremony at St. Michael's Church. Kimberly looked beautiful in her Chantilly lace and silk satin gown. It was a happy day for both this long-suffering former call girl and the dashing ISA agent!

THE WEDDING OF KAYLA BRADY AND STEVEN JOHNSON

Finally marrying his "Sweetness," Steven "Patch" Johnson arranged for Kayla Brady to have her childhood dream come true. The bride-to-be wanted to be married aboard a yacht in honor of the family fish market. Kayla, who had been temporarily deaf, entered the ceremony without being able to hear or speak. Miraculously, midvows, she heard everything the man of her dreams was saying. She surprised everybody when she said, "I do."

"I never dreamed of sharing my very soul. I dreamed of sharing my thoughts. I never dreamed someone could hear me without words. In my darkest trouble, in my coldest silence, I looked for you, and you were there. I am yours, Steve. Forever. I love you."

— Kayla Brady

THE WEDDING OF ADRIENNE JOHNSON AND JUSTIN KIRIAKIS

After a tortured romance filled with stops and starts, and twists and turns, star-crossed lovers Justin Kiriakis and Adrienne Johnson traveled to Greece with the Kiriakis family in tow for a bilingual Greek Orthodox wedding. This marked a new beginning for the down-on-her-luck bride and the former playboy.

THE WEDDING OF MARLENA EVANS AND ROMAN BRADY

Roman and Marlena finally tied the knot in February of 1983. Much like their courtship, the ceremony was full of heart-stopping danger and heart-tugging romance. After Tom Horton escorted Marlena down the aisle, Doug Williams sang "Serenade." During the performance, Stefano's hit man prepared to shoot Roman from the balcony of the church. However, Eugene Bradford discovered the sniper just in time and was able to warn the guests below. The assassin rushed off but Eugene and Chris Kositchek managed to apprehend the man. Marlena demanded to know what was going on, but Roman insisted he would explain later. After a brief tiff, the couple began the ceremony again. Roman and Marlena exchanged vows, then Doug sang their special song, "Up Where We Belong." After they placed the wedding rings on each other's fingers, they then took turns reciting poetic words by Johann Wolfgang von Goethe. Then the minister proudly pronounced Roman and Marlena husband and wife!

BACK
JENNIFER

SAME FLOWERS & LEAVES AT BACK

SATIN
FABRIC FLOWERS & LEAVES

Jennifer's vows to Jack
written by *Days of our Lives* Staff Writer Maura Penders

The Journey

Now we will feel no rain,
For each of us will be shelter to each other.
And now we will feel no cold,
For each of us will be warmth to each other.
Now there is no loneliness.
We are two bodies, but there is one life before us and one home.
When evening falls, I'll look to you and there you'll be.
And I'll take your hand and you'll take mine.
And we'll turn together and we'll look to the road we traveled to reach this,
The hour of our happiness.
It stretches far behind us, and our future lies ahead.
A long and winding road where every turning means discovery.
All the hopes, new laughter, shared tears,
The adventure has just begun.

Bloom 91

THE WEDDING OF JENNIFER HORTON AND JACK DEVERAUX

It's only fitting that Jack Deveraux and his bride Jennifer Horton married at Salem's Wild West Arena when they tied the knot on July 2, 1991. "The adventure was there and it was fun," says Matthew Ashford (Jack). "The whole day was a romp. Jack and Jennifer had fun adventures and then they got married in the sun."

"I was literally sewn into the back of my dress," recalls Melissa Reeves (Jennifer). "It ripped while we were doing a stunt. They asked us not to squint, but the sun was right in our eyes! Our characters got married at a time when our show traveled to all these beautiful locations. We thought, 'We can't wait to see where we are going!' But then we found out our wedding was shooting at Universal Studios, right down the street! By the time the shooting day was over, we realized it was a perfect place for Jack and Jennifer. It wouldn't have been right if we'd been off in some exotic locale."

"Jack's mind was always spinning," Reeves offers as to what made Jennifer good for him. "She would grab his thoughts and filter them. Matt brought this wonderful quality of humor to our coupling. It was a pairing I don't think that the show had planned, but it worked."

Ashford notes, "If things got difficult or awkward with couples, the writers would introduce another guy or girl who'd threaten the stability of the pair. But Jack and Jen could always threaten their pairing just by being who they were."

Jack and Jennifer married at Salem's Wild West Arena (taped at Universal Studios). A nervous Jack developed hysterical laryngitis the day before and when no one could find him the day of the wedding, some wondered if he had gotten cold feet. But Jack had been knocked into a well by one of the stunt men, only to have Alice, Carly, and Jennifer fight back. Once Jack regained consciousness, the wedding went off without a hitch with Bill Horton (Edward Mallory) returning to walk his daughter down the aisle. Jennifer read a beautiful poem called "The Journey" as part of her vows.

THE WEDDING OF MARLENA EVANS AND JOHN BLACK

In a day that many thought would never come, John Black and Marlena Evans married on July 5, 1999.

The couple made sure to involve their children as part of their ceremony, in addition to Sami serving as maid of honor and Eric being the best man.

Marlena and John likened their kids to a garden. Each was assigned a flower and asked to place it into a bouquet.

First, Marlena said that her and John's daughter, Belle, was "our daisy, our sunshine."

Next, John said that his son, Brady, with the late Isabella, was like a sunflower, "bold and adventurous."

Citing the potential for Sami's heart to be "huge and generous," Marlena and John assigned Sami a rose.

Next, John told Eric he was a "snapdragon" because he's headstrong and smart.

Lastly, Carrie was given an orchid to place in the bouquet, because they're both beautiful and fragile. "We can't claim her genetically," Marlena acknowledged, "but we raised her together. She will always be the child of our hearts."

LT. BLUE SATIN —
TRAIN OF METALLIC NET
MATTEL - DOLL

THE MARLENA COLLECTOR DOLL

Through the years, *Days of our Lives* connected with the audience in many ways and on many different levels. One of the most special times was in 1999 when Dr. Marlena Evans (played by Deidre Hall) was immortalized in a BARBIE® Collector Doll by Mattel, wearing a wedding dress designed by *Days of our Lives* costume designer, Richard Bloore.

Liz Chandler and Neil Curtis

Anna Fredericks and Tony DiMera

EMILY'S DIARY

Steve and Kayla were given an old mansion as a gift from Nick Corelli. In the attic, they found a trunk containing Civil War-era clothes and a diary of a young woman named Emily. As Steve and Kayla read the diary, they imagined themselves as Emily and her lover, Gideon, who shared a sweeping romance during the Civil War. Their tale came to a tragic end when Gideon was killed, leaving Emily pregnant with their child.

Months later, Kayla and Steve travelled to Charleston, South Carolina and visited spots where Emily and Gideon's love story took place. Kayla discovered Emily's second diary, in which it was revealed that Gideon was still alive. Steve and Kayla finished reading the compelling tale during a surprise picnic Steve set up to celebrate their wedding anniversary. They learned that Emily tracked Gideon to a prison camp where he was to be executed—but he was saved when the war ended. Kayla cried tears of joy as she read of Emily and Gideon's beautiful outdoor wedding.

"I never thought I could have somebody in my life that could make me so happy... make me feel so alive.... I love you, Hope."
—Bo

"And standing here in front of all of these people... I give you my life... and all my love... now and for all eternity. Oh Bo, I love you..."
—Hope

THE WEDDING OF
HOPE ALICE WILLIAMS AND BEAUREGARD AURELIUS BRADY

Just as you would imagine, Bo Brady and Hope Williams' trip to the altar was not an easy one. In fact, the nuptials featured a wedding crashing assassin and the newlyweds spent their wedding night in jail. However, in a beautiful ceremony in front of family, friends, and British nobility the young couple made it official.

Hope's wedding dress featured a 10-foot train made of silk satin and silk tulle. Bo and Hope were so popular that the series chose real-life fans to fill the pews of the church enabling them to watch the wedding of their favorite couple.

THE SURPRISE 50TH WEDDING ANNIVERSARY CELEBRATION OF ALICE AND TOM HORTON

Tom and Alice thought they were going to enjoy a small, quiet dinner together to celebrate their Golden Wedding Anniversary on March 7, 1980. They were at a table for two and then noticed Mickey and Maggie "coincidentally" dining nearby. Soon, it became apparent that pretty much the entire Horton clan had shown up to celebrate Tom and Alice's anniversary.

Left to right are Tom, Tommy, Hope, Marie, Alice, Laura, Trish, Bill, David, Mike, Doug, Margo, Julie, Mickey, and Maggie. Doug sang to his wife's grandparents their love song, "Always," as he walked the microphone around inviting family members to join in and sing a few bars.

It was rare for so many of Tom and Alice's children, grandchildren, and great-grandchildren to all be in Salem at the same time. Tom and Alice were so touched that the family gathered to share this once-in-a-lifetime milestone with them.

On *Days of our Lives*, when the officiating party says during the long-awaited union of two of your favorite characters: "If there be anyone present who may know why this couple should not be legally wed, let them speak now or forever hold their peace," it's a safe bet that someone will burst through the church, stand up in the pews, pass out at the altar, reveal a shocking secret, and rain on the couple's nuptials! Many duos have suffered "wedding interruptus" through the years, but one character in particular, Sami Brady, has the distinction of having the most weddings in Salem go bust, thanks in part to her lies and deceit. Below are some classic "interruptions":

- Hope Williams to Larry Welch—After Hope agreed to marry duplicitous DA Larry Welch, all she could think about on her wedding day was Bo Brady. Bo saved the day and swooped into the church, whisking Hope away, and another bride came down the aisle to marry Larry… Howie Hoffstedder!

- Carly Manning to Bo Brady—Just as these lovebirds were about to say "I do", in burst Lawrence Alamain with the revelation that he fathered Carly's son Nikki, who had just been kidnapped by Vivian.

- Sami Brady and Austin Reed—Pretending to have amnesia, and lying about the fact that she was pregnant with his child, Sami got a duped Austin to the altar. But Sami's older sister Carrie showed up in the nick of time with proof that Lucas was the baby's father, not Austin. Carrie finished off the ceremony breakup by punching Sami in the face for keeping her and Austin apart with her deception.

- Sami Brady and Lucas Horton—Sami had been causing trouble while masquerading as a man ("Stan"). Armed with the knowledge of "Stan's" true identity, Kate headed to the church dressed like "Stan" and Sami fainted. It was game over.

- Sami Brady and EJ DiMera—As Sami was about to wed EJ, Rafe busted up the ceremony just before the couple was pronounced man and wife with the fact that… EJ staged little Sydney's kidnapping and death to get revenge on Sami for keeping the child a secret.

- Kristen DiMera and Brady Black—Marlena unknowingly played the wrong DVD which broke up her stepson's wedding to her archrival. Attendees in the church watched in horror as a clip played of Kristen having sex with Father Eric Brady. It was later revealed she actually drugged and raped Eric to get him into this compromising position.

Wedding Interruptus

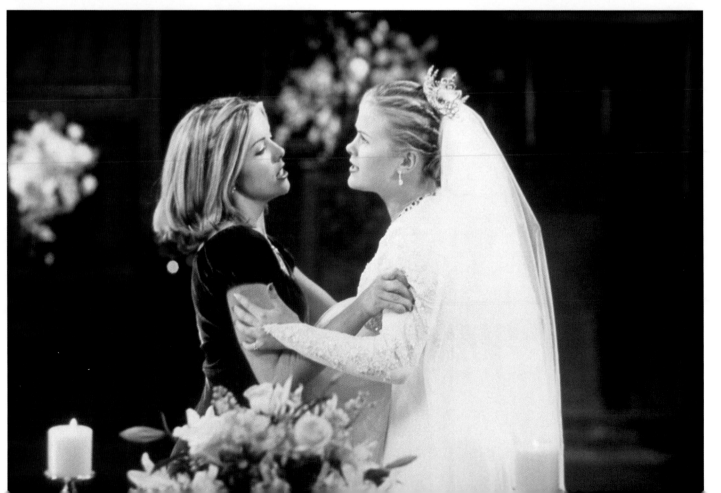

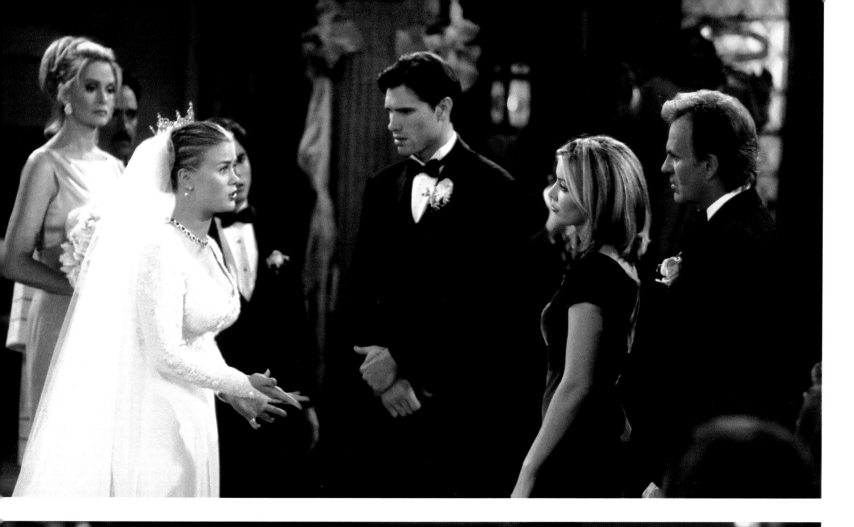

THE WEDDING OF HOPE WILLIAMS AND LARRY WELCH

Hope allowed herself to be charmed by aspiring Larry Welch. Believing Bo didn't love her, she was anxious to try to move on with her life. However, she was unaware that Bo had gone undercover to save the life of his brother Roman. Surrounded by family and friends, Hope braced herself to marry Larry, and even Grandma Alice told Hope it wasn't too late to change her mind. Alice knew that Hope desperately loved Bo.

Just in the nick of time, Bo showed up—burst into the bride's room—saying he was there to claim his woman. Alice helped the duo escape and conspired with Bo's pal Howie Hoffstedder, who donned a wedding gown and veil to pose as Hope. Larry was in for quite a surprise when he lifted "Hope's" veil.

UNHAPPILY EVER AFTER

Larry refused to give up on making Hope his wife, especially after being publicly humiliated at the altar! Soon after Hope realized Bo's love for her was indeed genuine, she was forcibly taken by thugs working for Maxwell Hathaway. They informed Hope in no uncertain terms that if she didn't marry Larry, then Bo would be killed! This time, it was Hope's turn to make the sacrifice. She begrudgingly tied the knot with Larry in order to keep her true love safe. In public, Hope played the dutiful wife, but in private, she had no problem telling Larry exactly how she felt!

Their union ended in spectacular fashion after Bo, Hope, and the other plane crash survivors returned from a deserted island, where they had been stranded for weeks. Hope was stunned to learn her "dear" husband had been elected Lieutenant Governor in her absence—he won by playing up the role of grieving widow. Furious, Hope stood in front of a crowd of news reporters and announced her marriage was a complete sham! She revealed she and Larry had been forced to marry by a cartel led by none other than Stefano DiMera! DiMera had planned on using Larry as a political puppet. This bombshell caused a huge uproar. Eventually, Larry was forced to resign in disgrace, and Hope got the divorce she so desperately wanted, leaving her free to be with her true love, Bo.

THE BACHELORETTE PARTY OF CARRIE BRADY

At Carrie's bachelorette party, the men from Austin's bachelor party showed up and crashed it. Luckily for the ladies, all the guys pretended to be male strippers… and the gals got an eyeful!

Mr. and Mrs. Shawn Brady

request the honor of your presence

at the marriage of their granddaughter

Carrie

to

Mr. Austin Reed

Thursday, the twenty-seventh of July

at three o'clock in the afternoon

St. Luke's Church

Salem

THE WEDDING OF CARRIE BRADY AND AUSTIN REED

Sami drugs and sleeps with Austin, who thinks he's making love to Carrie. Austin gently tells Sami he doesn't have feelings for her. Humiliated, she flees town. Austin then confesses to Carrie he had a one-night stand but she insists she didn't want to know with whom. Austin then proposes to Carrie.

Carrie and Austin's wedding day arrives. Mickey spots Sami lurking outside the church and brings her inside. The family is relieved she's back, and Sami puts on a bridesmaid dress. As John begins the ceremony, Sami "faints." To everyone's shock, she "accidentally" reveals she's pregnant! Carrie and Marlena take her to the bride's room while Austin freaks out. Sami finally reveals Austin is the father. Austin is forced to admit he slept with Sami, and Carrie slaps him and calls off the wedding.

THE WEDDING OF CARLY MANNING AND BO BRADY

Carly and Lawrence had discovered that Nikki was their child (Vivian had been raising him). They decided to keep the news a secret. However, at Carly's wedding to Bo, Lawrence rushed in and interrupted it announcing that Vivian had kidnapped their son! Bo was shocked that Carly had kept such a huge secret from him and the wedding was postponed.

THE WEDDING OF SAMANTHA BRADY AND EJ DIMERA

In an elaborate revenge plot, a scorned Sami set out to make EJ pay for his affair with the younger Abigail Deveraux. For months, EJ and Abby were able to think their tryst was behind them, but think again! Sami knew for months, and waited for the right time for some payback! Just after Sami and EJ exchanged wedding vows, EJ was arrested for tax evasion. Turns out, it was a well-orchestrated plot from Sami and Kate to gain control of DiMera Enterprises, and really got EJ where it hurts. A gloating and vengeful Sami showed up at EJ's jail cell and laid a bombshell on him. She knew about his affair... and gained control of his company.

THE WEDDING OF KRISTEN DIMERA AND BRADY BLACK

Kristen thought she would be able to finally get hitched to Brady Black, much to the chagrin of Marlena Evans! However, Marlena inadvertently showed a DVD at the wedding of Kristen having sex with her son, Father Eric Brady… the man that was officiating the union! As the guests gasped, and watched this "sexcapade," Eric realized Kristen had drugged and raped him. Needless to say, the wedding was called off!

An all-out brawl between Brady and Father Eric ensued, since Brady believed Eric set out to have lustful sex with his bride-to-be!

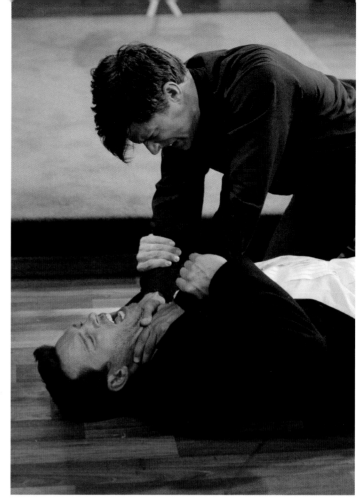

UNSINKABLE WOMEN

Salem is known for its strong, independent women who are determined to succeed not only in business, but also in love. These remarkable ladies are fiercely protective of their families and have no problem standing up for what they believe—messing with them is definitely at your own peril! Occasionally their passion and drive can get them into trouble, yet they always find a way to persevere. The following "unsinkable" women have been a driving force in Salem for years:

- Kate Roberts
- Samantha Brady
- Julie Olson
- Maggie Simmons
- Hope Williams
- Marlena Evans
- Jennifer Horton
- Caroline Brady
- Nicole Walker
- Abigail Deveraux

KATE ROBERTS

Kate is a survivor. She has overcome an abusive husband, a plane crash that left her stranded in the middle of the ocean, and even lung cancer. She's had to scratch and claw her way to the top more than once in her lifetime. And really, the top is where she belongs. She's a ruthless, respected businesswoman who can tangle with the best of them—as she proved when she and Sami teamed up to steal DiMera Enterprises right out from under Stefano and EJ's noses. Kate is one woman you never want to cross.

SAMANTHA BRADY

Yes, Sami can be vindictive and manipulative, but she is also a fiercely protective mother and a deeply loving partner. If she has your back, you know she'll do anything for you—even if that means she has to lie, cheat, or steal. Or switch paternity tests—she's really good at that. She also excels at walking down the aisle, running cosmetics empires, and disguising herself as a man. When EJ broke her heart by cheating on her with Abigail, Sami didn't just break down and cry—she got even.

JULIE OLSON

Brazen, strong-willed, and confident, Julie has never been afraid to go after what she wants—even when the whole world was against her. Case in point: after giving up her son, David, for adoption, Julie regretted her decision and set out to find him, despite the protests of her family. She succeeded and was overjoyed when she regained custody of her son. Julie was also a successful businesswoman who never had any trouble facing down the likes of Stefano DiMera or Victor Kiriakis. Now that she's a little wiser and a little less impetuous, Julie often uses the lessons she learned from her trouble making past to counsel the next generation of young women who have the same fire and ambition as she did.

MAGGIE SIMMONS

Having lost her parents at a young age, Maggie ran an entire farm all on her own—even while being dependent on crutches. After risky surgery, Maggie regained full use of her legs and proved nothing could hold her back. Maggie also battled through an alcohol addiction, and then became a supportive AA sponsor to people like Lucas and Brady. Over the years, Maggie has also run several successful businesses, including the restaurants Tuscany and Chez Rouge. While Maggie is loving and kind, she's no pushover—after all, it takes a tough woman to put up with Victor Kiriakis.

HOPE WILLIAMS

Hope may have started out as a spoiled princess but she eventually became one of the bravest and most brilliant detectives on the Salem police force. In between solving crimes, Hope often finds herself in the middle of outrageous adventures—like battling look-alike Princess Gina or searching for a cure in the middle of a dangerous jungle. And while she's sometimes "holding out for a hero," she's proven throughout the years that she certainly doesn't need one. Hope does just fine on her own, thank you. Earring from www.hopefaithmiracles.com By Kristian Alfonso.

MARLENA EVANS

As a testament to Marlena's incredible strength, she has battled and triumphed over such adversaries as Stefano, Kristen, and even the Devil himself! She's been possessed, locked in a cage, hypnotized into carrying out a killing spree, and committed to a sanitarium by her own twin sister, yet Marlena remains as poised, kindhearted, and compassionate as she's ever been. With everything she does, Marlena carries herself with class and dignity. She's known as not only a brilliant and revered psychiatrist but also a loving wife, mother, and friend.

JENNIFER HORTON

Sweet Jennifer was once a rebellious teenager who ran away from home. Although she has matured and grown into a responsible, caring woman, her spunkiness still remains. When Jennifer found her archenemy, Eve, in bed with her son, JJ, all hell broke loose. After all, feisty Jennifer is never one to back down from a fight, especially in the pursuit of truth or justice. This made her a successful investigative reporter and a good friend to those in need. She once even proved her loyalty to Carly by marrying Lawrence in her place.

CAROLINE BRADY

Caroline is the backbone of the Brady clan—and for good reason. She's a woman who's made mistakes (her affair with Victor) and then learned from them. As a result, she won't judge family members in need, but rather, she listens with compassion. Most importantly, she always lets troublemakers like granddaughters Sami and Theresa know they are loved no matter what. Caroline has been especially brave in recent years as she's battled a neurological disease with grace and dignity.

NICOLE WALKER

Back in the day, Nicole was what you might call a gold digger. She agreed to dump Eric and marry Lucas when Kate offered her $5 million to help her son win custody of Will. However, Nicole evolved and overcame a lot of disappointments in life (including two miscarriages) to become the confident, motivated woman she is today. Not that she doesn't still make mistakes—but now she tends to follow with her heart and not her wallet.

ABIGAIL DEVERAUX

Abigail has overcome many hurdles in life, starting when she was an infant and survived a battle with aplastic anemia. As she grew up all over the world, she had to deal with an unstable family life due to her parents' constant breaking up and reuniting. As a teenager, she rebelled against Jennifer and later made some ill-advised choices in going after married men Austin and EJ. However, Abigail has matured into a kind and caring young woman, who is fiercely loyal to her family, especially her mom and brother. She still makes mistakes, but owns them and tries to do better. Once her affair with EJ was exposed, Abigail became a much stronger and more confident person while enduring Sami's vengeful wrath. It's quite an accomplishment if you can go up against Sami Brady and not only walk away unscathed, but also get a few hits in there yourself.

Lexie Carver on the town with her mother, Celeste Perrault.

The men of Salem can do it all—rescue damsels in distress, ride motorcycles, fly planes, defeat Stefano DiMera's plan to rule the world, and make it home in time for dinner—all while flashing a perfect smile and flexing a well-defined bicep. Here are six of the most tireless leading men from 50 years of *Days of our Lives*.

Bo Brady

A former merchant marine, Bo fights passionately for his family and the woman he loves. Bo knows he has to do the right thing even when it means putting his own happiness aside. He's cared for many women—Carly, Billie—but *Days of our Lives* fans know that at the end of the day he's a one-woman man, completely devoted to Hope, whom he affectionately calls "Fancy Face."

Steve "Patch" Johnson

Patch has never lost the rough edges he developed living on the wrong side of the tracks, but his love for Kayla Brady has allowed him to endure many hardships. He's cheated death, learned sign language, and come up with the most endearing nickname for his lady love—"Sweetness"—that we've ever heard.

Abe Carver

Abe's the rock of Salem. He's the guy people turn to when they need a sympathetic ear, strong shoulder, or the strong arm of the law. A single dad to his son, Theo, now that his beloved Lexie is gone, Abe is known as the Mayor of Salem—even when he's not officially holding the office!

John Black

Fate throws a lot at John Black and each time his true origin becomes more mysterious than ever. Whether he's a priest performing an exorcism, fighting Stefano, trying to escape a guillotine, or battling paralysis or a drug addiction, John is ready to fight to the finish. His motivation? Why, it's his beloved "Doc"! (Who else?)

Jack Deveraux

Jack Deveraux has won a lot of hearts—especially the one that belongs to his wife Jennifer—by being zany, funny, and honest. Jack doesn't always initially make the right choice, but the hero in him eventually does the right thing. He may be gone—but Jack will never, ever be forgotten.

Lucas Horton

This reformed bad boy knows that a mischievous grin can get people to overlook a lot. Over the years, however, Lucas has matured. He does the right thing. He's a supportive dad to his children, and maintains a cordial relationship with Sami, his ex-wife. She's not his only former spouse. Lucas has been wed to four different women and has had his share of flings. He has yet to find his true soul mate, but he's not giving up. He is, after all, unstoppable!

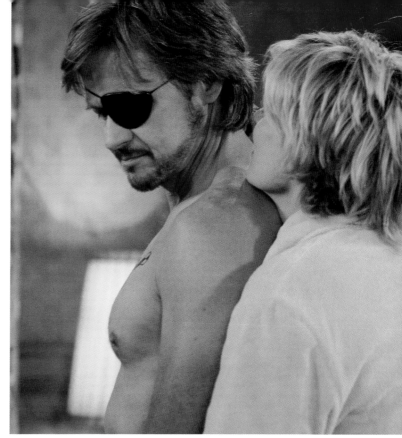

Every hero needs a worthy adversary, and in Salem, there's never a short supply of diabolical villains willing to do battle. Yet most of these troublemakers aren't completely evil, and that's why they're so fascinating. They have a tendency to go to extremes to get what they want, often times employing some "creative" tactics to do so. The following rogues gallery consists of people who have locked their enemies in secret rooms, sentenced them to death by guillotine, and even buried them alive!

Stefano DiMera—No one has committed more unthinkable crimes than Stefano. Over the years, he's kidnapped half the town of Salem, helped switch several babies, and used brainwashing or microchips to control the minds of John, Steve, Hope, Vivian, and more. The one crime Stefano has not committed? He's never directly killed anyone—he simply has others do the dirty deed.

Andre DiMera—Andre was so maniacal and evil, he's probably considered the most lethal DiMera aside from Stefano. Andre went on a killing spree as the Salem Slasher in the 1980s. Decades later, he got back in the serial killer game when he masterminded the Salem Stalker plot. He also cut out a part of Benjy's liver and then tossed him in a Dumpster.

Megan Hathaway—Desperate to win back her ex-boyfriend, Bo, Megan tricked him into believing they had a child together. When that didn't work, she tried to electrocute Hope in a hot tub. She certainly took after her father, Stefano.

Kristen DiMera—What crime hasn't Kristen committed? She faked her pregnancy to keep John, she tried to kill Marlena, and she sold Susan Banks into white slavery. Perhaps her worst offense was raping Father Eric. Or maybe it was stealing Theresa's baby right from her womb. Or maybe…

Peter Blake—Peter loved Jennifer so much, he did just about anything to keep her—which included kidnapping, murder, and using toxic paint to drive her poor mother, Laura, insane. Strangely enough, Jennifer did not find all this endearing and finally dumped him.

EJ DiMera—EJ excelled at being a true DiMera. He covered all the basics—kidnapping, murder, etc.—with ease. But EJ really went the extra mile by brainwashing Steve, forcing Sami to have sex in exchange for saving Lucas' life, faking Sydney's death, and replacing Rafe with an imposter. Thankfully, EJ toned things down once he and Sami fell in love.

Victor Kiriakis—Victor has mellowed in recent years, but this Greek crime lord used to be just as lethal as Stefano back in the day. He ran a drug and pornography ring, and he had no qualms about eliminating enemies—which at times included his own son, Bo!

Lawrence Alamain—Debonair and ruthless, Lawrence perpetrated heinous crimes in his obsessive pursuit of Dr. Carly Manning—including imprisoning Alice and raping Jennifer. He was also responsible for Steve's apparent death. After leaving Salem with Carly, he developed a disease which caused him to go insane. He became abusive and even forced Carly to give up her illegitimate daughter, Melanie Jonas, at birth.

Vivian Alamain—When Vivian first arrived in Salem, she shot a man who was holding Lawrence at gunpoint, then nonchalantly stepped over his dead body to greet her beloved nephew. Vivian's stunts only got bolder—and crazier—after that. She buried Carly alive and tormented her via radio. She also stole Victor and Kate's embryo and had it implanted in herself!

Ernesto Toscano—Ernesto was a wealthy businessman who had a fondness for magic tricks. In two extreme acts of revenge, he poisoned both his wife, Loretta (she died), and Isabella (she survived). He also invited his enemies on a "Cruise of Deception," which ended in Hope's "death."

Orpheus—This former ISA agent sought revenge against Roman (actually John) by playing all sorts of mental games with him. He kidnapped Marlena and staged her death more than once.

Clyde Weston—Clyde is a big-time drug dealer from the small town of Poplar Bluff. He attempted to squeeze EJ out of the Salem drug trade, resulting in EJ's death. He then went up against Victor and had Victor's nephew, Sonny, stabbed in order to send a message. In the past, Clyde was also abusive towards Jordan and Ben—not to mention the fact that he took sexual advantage of his step-daughter.

Jake Kositchek—Aka the Salem Strangler, the younger brother of Chris Kositchek, dumped by Jessica Fallon's alter ego, Angel, he became one of Salem's most infamous serial killers. Jake's victims included Mary Anderson and Marlena's twin sister, Samantha.

Harper Deveraux—Harper was a smooth politician who eventually was unmasked as the Riverfront Knifer. He killed several women, including Janice Barnes, and also kidnapped sisters Kayla and Kimberly.

Curtis Reed—Kate's abusive husband kidnapped their children, Austin and Billie, and led Kate to believe they were dead. Curtis then sexually abused his daughter and got her hooked on drugs. Curtis was hated by so many that when he was murdered in 1994, there was a long list of suspects.

Linda Patterson—Linda was Mickey's legal secretary, and the two had a torrid affair. In order to trap Mickey, Linda claimed her daughter, Melissa, was his child. She later tried to drive Melissa insane to get her daughter's shares of Anderson Manufacturing.

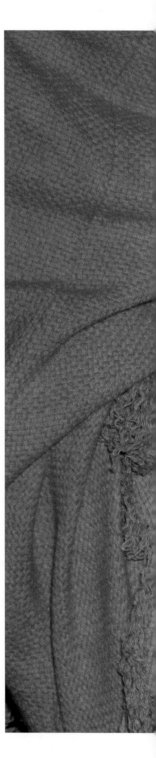

December 1994 - Strange Confessions

Dr. Marlena Evans was, by her own admission, at a low point in her life. She and her husband, Roman Brady, had divorced after he learned of her affair with another man. In a moment of full disclosure, I must admit I, John Black, was that man. Marlena started to behave strangely, and no one seemed to know why. She was known as a kind-hearted, respected psychiatrist – yet she started giving questionable advice to her step-daughter, Carrie Brady. She was also drawn towards the moon and was inexplicably tired all the time. What we didn't realize was Stefano DiMera was entering her bedroom at night and escorting her through the armoire to a strange and fantastical setting. Marlena believed these nightly outings were merely dreams, but the excursions soon made her vulnerable to an evil more powerful than Stefano. Unsettling events began happening around Salem. The Horton Christmas tree went up in flames, while presents were destroyed at the Horton Center and the Brady Pub. St. Luke's Church was vandalized, and Hope Williams (going by the name Gina at the time) was attacked. The "Desecrator" was waging an unholy war against Salem. No one could have suspected Marlena was the culprit. We now know that it was around this time that she started levitating in her bedroom, her eyes glowing an unearthly yellow. She once told me she saw a beast in her bedroom. I wish now I had taken her claims more seriously.

January 1995 - Destructive Behavior

Marlena secretly continued to wreck havoc on the town. She loosened the screws of St. Luke's chandelier, which came crashing down during the almost-wedding of Bo Brady and Billie Reed. She also chloroformed Kristen DiMera and painted pentagrams on her naked body. In one of her most fiendish plots yet, Marlena transformed herself to look like Kristen and tried to seduce me.

February 1995 - Heinous Crimes and Public Nudity

Marlena set fire to St. Luke's, but soon the Salem PD found evidence she was the desecrator. No one could understand why she would commit such heinous crimes, but Celeste Perrault confided to Stefano that she believed Marlena was possessed. Later, Marlena stunned the entire town when she sauntered into Bo and Billie's wedding reception completely naked. She seemed to be in a trance and was admitted into the hospital.

March 1995 - Hospitalized Under Observation

Marlena remained in the hospital as doctors tried to figure out what was wrong with her. Of course, they could find no natural cause.

April 1995 - Satan Reveals Himself

The Devil finally revealed himself to Celeste, while Kristen and Father Jansen began to suspect Marlena was possessed.

May 1995 - Otherworldly Occurrences

Marlena tried her best to fight the demon inside her, but it was a losing battle. She sent a swarm of bees to attack the guests at Carrie and Austin Reed's engagement party, where Shawn Brady, Sr. was injured. She also turned into a jaguar and attacked holy scholars in the park. That night, an otherworldly meteor shower began to rain down... and I witnessed a horrific sight I will never forget. Stefano, Kristen, Father Francis, and I rushed to Marlena's penthouse – and were shocked to find Marlena levitating above her bed! We began an exorcism as quickly as we could. We held several sessions, and Caroline Brady also participated. The Devil did everything he could to thwart our attempts to save Marlena's soul. He even tried to play on my emotions by appearing as my dearly-departed wife, Isabella. But I saw through his tricks, and we continued our efforts.

June 1995 - Apparent Death After Attempted Exorcism

Alone with Marlena, Stefano was tricked into untying her bonds. The Devil then threw him off the balcony. Once Marlena was again secured to her bed, Dr. Mike Horton warned us she was too physically weak for our exorcism to continue. However, I made one last attempt to expel the demon from Marlena's body. The battle proved to be too much for her, and Marlena died. Or at least that's what we were led to believe.

July 1995 - Marlena's Soul Finally Saved

I was completely heartbroken and devastated over Marlena's death. I went to visit her body in the morgue – and was stunned when Marlena, still possessed, attacked me. After an intense struggle, during which I was briefly possessed myself, I called upon God's name and finally was able to cast out the Devil! Marlena's soul was saved.

I know many may find my account of this incident hard to believe. But I assure you, every word is true.
Good triumphed over Evil.

Faithfully,
Fr. John Black

EJ DIMERA AND ABE CARVER CAMPAIGN FOR MAYOR

In 2011, Abe started his campaign for re-election as the mayor of Salem. To everyone's surprise, EJ threw his hat into the ring. Lexie wasn't pleased her brother was running against her husband, and she warned EJ he'd better not do anything to hurt her family.

Abe hired Jennifer as his publicist, while EJ convinced Nicole to sign on as his campaign manager. The race quickly became heated and personal. Abe and Jennifer tried to keep things clean but realized Abe would lose if he didn't combat EJ's dirty tactics. Upon learning DiMera was going to get the questions to an important mayoral debate, Abe and Jennifer not only procured their own copy of the questions but also replaced EJ's with a fake set. After the debate, Abe was the clear winner. EJ and Nicole angrily accused him of cheating.

On election day, Abe pulled out a major victory. However, evidence of ballot tampering soon came to light, and EJ was eventually declared Salem's new mayor. His first order of business was to arrest Jennifer and Abe for electoral fraud. The charges were eventually dropped—the true culprit was Stefano, who had secretly rigged the election so Abe would win.

JJ Deveraux

Who knew picking up trash was a good way to meet girls? #CrushedOut #HotGirlSighting

Paige Larson

He told me I'm beautiful. #Blush #FirstKiss

Paige Larson

@JD Can't wait 4U to meet my mom!

JJ Deveraux

@PL Ur mom is so… not what I expected.

Paige Larson

That awkward moment when u realize ur mom and ur bf's mom are mortal enemies.

JJ Deveraux

Just so everyone out there knows, I did NOT get drunk and hook up with some girl. #SetUp

Paige Larson

What do u do when the boy u love pulls away and u have no idea why?

JJ Deveraux

Sometimes I think I'm destined to follow in my dad's footsteps. And not in a good way.

Paige Larson

Major fight tonight. Think it's over. :-(

JJ Deveraux

Made the mother of all mistakes 2night. #EpicLifeFail

Paige Larson

Came back from CA to surprise BF for XMAS. He broke up w/me. No explanation. Happy holidays! #WTH

— text by Ryan Quan, Staff Writer, *Days of our Lives*

EVE DONOVAN AND JJ DEVERAUX'S AFFAIR

In his senior year of high school, JJ Deveraux fell head over heels for good girl Paige Larson. They embarked on a sweet romance… which came to a screeching halt one night when they had a huge misunderstanding. Upset, JJ ended up seeking comfort from another woman—Paige's mom, Eve Donovan!

Paige overheard Eve and JJ discussing their affair, and when JJ threw her a surprise birthday party, Paige angrily confronted him in front of family and friends. JJ was devastated, and Paige swore she would never, ever forgive him or her mother for as long as she lived.

The "knight in shining armor," whose courage and bravery in the face of adversity make women swoon, can come in many forms on *Days of our Lives*. Throughout the decades spies, cops, and former bad boys going undercover for the greater good, have been paramount to many umbrella and wildly successful stories, and more. From cops Roman Brady, Bo Brady, Rafe Hernandez, and Abe Carver to ISA agents Shane Donovan, John Black, and Steve "Patch" Johnson, these guys were put to the test, whether it be for their brains or their brawn! While these tough, larger-than-life gents were battling the bad guys, their wives or girlfriends patiently awaited their return each night, each month, or sometimes years if they were away on a top secret mission!

- Cop Shop
- Cop Undercover
- ISA Agents

COP SHOP

- **Roman Brady**—This top cop first appeared on the show to watch over and guard Marlena Evans from a serial killer. While they spatted, and he slept on the floor each night, soon the two fell madly in love. Roman's archenemy, Stefano DiMera, had other plans for him—he shot Roman, and then Roman went over a cliff to his "death"! Years later Roman was revealed to be alive! Now he is top commanding officer at the Salem PD, and watching over the town and its residents.

- **Bo Brady**—Following in his older brother Roman's footsteps, Bo became a cop too. While Stefano DiMera and Ernesto Toscano wreaked havoc on the lives of the Brady family and their loved ones, it was Bo who would ride to the rescue to save Hope, Carly, or anyone else he loved from harm's way.

- **Rafe Hernandez**—Federal Agent Hernandez came to Salem to guard Sami Brady, as she was in the Witness Protection Program, and the two eventually fell in love. Later Rafe saved Sami from marrying his archnemesis EJ, armed with the truth through his investigative skills that EJ was behind her daughter's kidnapping.

- **Abe Carver**—Wanting to find justice, Abe Carver came on to the Salem scene as a police officer to investigate Anna Fredericks' claim that she was sold into white slavery. He became good friends with Roman Brady, and they continue to rid the streets of Salem of crime and wrongdoing to this day. At one time, he was the mayor of the city, and has been the Salem PD police commissioner.

- **Hope Williams**—Hope accidentally applied to the Salem PD when she signed the wrong form at the station. Bo teased her mercilessly about it, unable to imagine the "spoiled little princess" as an officer. Hope set out to prove Bo wrong, and so she decided to go through with training. She eventually became one of the top detectives on the force.

- **Lexie Brooks**—While acting as a decoy in the Riverfront Knifer case, Lexie cut her hand in a brawl and feared her police career was finished. Officer Abe Carver encouraged her not to quit. They eventually fell in love and were married for twenty years. After helping a vigilante in cleaning up the streets of Salem, Lexie was kicked off the force. Though she later had a chance to be reinstated, she decided to pursue a career as a doctor.

- **Billie Reed**—With her past of drugs and prostitution, Billie wanted to change her life and put those behind bars who had wronged her and other women. After working undercover with Bo, with whom she fell in love, she eventually decided to enter the police academy and work for the right side of the law.

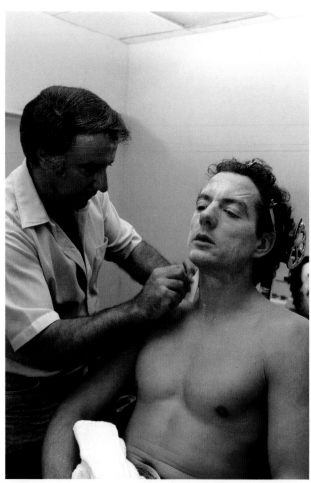

COP UNDERCOVER

Wayne Northrop as cop Roman Brady gets a makeover to go undercover as Mr. Snow to bust a local cocaine ring. Lynn Herring, Wayne's wife, documents the transformation.

Dossiers of Salem's Most Famous ISA (International Security Alliance) Agents

AGENT: Shane Donovan

BACKGROUND: Born and raised in England. Has a twin brother named Andrew Donovan III. Was mentored by Levinia "Peachie" Peach.

FAMOUS MISSIONS: Came to Salem posing as Larry Welch's butler to bring down Stefano DiMera. Prevented DiMera from collecting the three prisms. Helped put a stop to terrorist known as the Dragon. Tried to bring down Victor Kiriakis. Eliminated Alfred Jericho. Investigated a deadly virus that was killing ISA agents (linked to Kiriakis and Lawrence Alamain).

SPECIAL SKILLS: Expert marksman and fencer. Can diffuse bombs.

AGENT: John Black

ALIASES: Forrest Alamain, John Stevens, The Pawn, Roman Brady, Ryan Brady

BACKGROUND: Ancestry is a mystery. Adopted by the Alamain family then brainwashed by Stefano DiMera to be a mercenary and his "pawn." Was at various points thought to be Roman Brady, an art thief, a priest, and the son of Colleen Brady and Santo DiMera.

FAMOUS MISSIONS: Assisted the ISA in tracking down missing bonds in Stockholm and taking down Orpheus (as Roman Brady). Tried to bring down Tony DiMera. A few notable non-ISA missions: Hunting down a cure for Roman Brady in the jungle. Rescuing Dr. Marlena Evans from Stefano DiMera's underground Parisian lair.

SPECIAL SKILLS: Highly trained at hand-to-hand combat. Experienced pilot. Performs exorcisms.

AGENT: Steven Earl Johnson

ALIASES: Patch, Brother Daniel Lucas, Nick

BACKGROUND: Grew up in an orphanage. Was in the Merchant Marines. Lost left eye in a fight with Bo Brady.

FAMOUS MISSIONS: First official job was to track down a serial arsonist—the culprits turned **out** to be Reverend Saul Taylor and Alfred Jericho. Also assisted with the Orpheus Case.

SPECIAL SKILLS: Plays the harmonica. Knows sign language.

In the '80s, '90s, and into the new millennium, *Days of our Lives* delivered high stakes drama set against the backdrop of exciting locales, such as Venice, Italy, New Orleans, Louisiana, Paris, France, and more. Big sprawling stories comprised of many cast members was the order of the day, where *Days of our Lives* put many of its core characters in danger, and implanted them into an unraveling mystery story, a major event, or a shocking revelation that took the action out of the studio setting and on location. Even new sets were built. And then there were those secret underground tunnels or destinations… remember Aremid? (DiMera spelled backwards.) Here's a look at few of the most intense, thrill-a-minute cliffhanger story lines where action, love, and murder collided!

- Jungle Madness

- Three Prisms

- Cruise of Deception

- Flying Nun

- The Symbolic Mexican Wedding Adventure

- Stephanie's Rescue

- John and Marlena's Italian Wedding Adventure

High Adventure

JUNGLE MADNESS

John, Hope, Stefano, and Kristen all traveled to a jungle compound where they were introduced to Dr. Rolf, the man working on the cure for Roman. Dr. Rolf recognized Hope, but Stefano managed to warn him not to say anything to her. Hope ended up breaking into a storage room, which infuriated Stefano because there were things in that room, including a table, that could jog her memory of the missing four years of her life. Stefano promptly closed the room up with a high-tech lock. When Dr. Rolf finally finished his work, the vial containing it was dropped and the cure was lost. Dr. Rolf and Stefano told John and Hope that the only way to make another cure was for someone to brave the jungle and the natives to retrieve a special orchid. John volunteered to find the orchid, and Stefano manipulated things so Hope went with him. John and Hope grew close during their harrowing adventure (though John still loved Marlena and Hope still loved Bo). Hope and John found the orchid and John put it in his backpack, but a native knocked John off a cliff and Hope, Kristen, and Stefano thought he was killed. John's backpack was recovered, but the orchid was missing. Hope managed to find some of the orchid's seeds and Rolf made a cure using them. John later returned to the compound, but was poisoned by a native's dart. Dr. Rolf cured him as well and everyone left to go back to Salem. Later, Peter came to Dr. Rolf looking for a cure for Jungle Madness!

THREE PRISMS

Stefano DiMera was residing in a secret location carefully planning a way to retrieve three valuable prisms that were in the possession of Maxwell and Megan Hathaway. The prisms, he said, would cure his brain tumor. Although Stefano had faked his death, he was really suffering from an inoperable brain tumor. During this time, Megan Hathaway was revealed to be Stefano's daughter, not Maxwell's. The prisms were of great importance to Stefano. When the prisms were together and held underneath a laser, they revealed coded instructions to several breakthroughs in technology and science; one of these breakthroughs was how to operate on Stefano's type of tumor. The prisms had been designed by an American, but Communist scientist Victor Chorvat made them part of a Soviet plot called the "Triad Experiment." Unbeknownst to Stefano, Marlena and Eugene Bradford had discovered information about the Triad Experiment… and the location of his compound in Venezuela. Meanwhile, a Russian named Bronski successfully managed to smuggle the last prism out of the Soviet Union through an ice-skating troupe. When the troupe came to Salem, Stefano and his henchgirl Sonia made their way to the rafters above the ice rink. Just as they were going to escape through the roof and catch their helicopter, Marlena appeared brandishing a gun. Stefano was shot and dropped the prism, and eventually was believed to be dead in a fire that ignited.

CRUISE OF DECEPTION

This story arc was billed as a miniseries event in itself! It aired for a few weeks in July of 1990. The story included several of the show's most popular characters trapped aboard a cruise ship with a vengeful, evil Ernesto Toscano. The story took place aboard the *Loretta*, an ocean liner commandeered by Ernesto, named after his deceased wife. His main purpose in putting together the cruise was to exact revenge on all of his supposed enemies at one time. Invited on the cruise were Isabella Toscano, John Black (believed to be Roman), Bo Brady, Hope Brady, Jack Deveraux, Jennifer Horton, Julie Williams, and Ernesto's number one sworn enemy, Victor Kiriakis. Twisted Ernesto seemed to have a fetish for magic tricks, and enjoyed toying and terrorizing the passengers aboard!

THE FLYING NUN

Marie Horton was "unlucky in love," having fallen in love with her brother, Tommy, and later with the unscrupulous Alex Marshall, with whom she shared a "love" child. Upon entering a convent, Marie gave this daughter up for adoption. Years later both Alex and their daughter, Jessica, wound up in Salem.

En route to Montreal to obtain information about Jessica, Marie and Alex were involved in a plane crash. During this time, Alex realized he actually loved Marie… which later prompted great jealousy from his ex-wife Mary Anderson.

- Mary learned the truth about Jessica and made sure she found out too.

- Jessica developed a multiple personality disorder

- Marie stopped Jake from marrying Jessica aka "Angelique"

- Although Marie and Alex's renewed relationship failed, daughter Jessica managed to find happiness with Joshua Fallon

CARLY MANNING AND BO BRADY'S SYMBOLIC WEDDING ADVENTURE IN MEXICO

In a last ditch attempt to break up Bo and Carly, Victor faked his death and fled to Mexico to find a set of codices. Roman, John, and Marlena all traced their medals to a Mayan temple in Mexico. Roman, Marlena, Isabella, John, Bo, and Carly all went to Mexico in search of the truth where they found Victor Kiriakis chained in one of the temples. Eventually they made their way to a room in which Stefano DiMera was waiting for them. Using the medals, Stefano gained access to a set of codices which promised the holder power beyond imagination. Stefano also had a satchel which held the truth about John's past. Suddenly an earthquake occurred, setting off a volcano, and the temple began to crumble and fill with lava. Stefano threw the satchel into the fire and was then crushed and lost among the falling debris. John managed to recover the satchel, but the contents were badly burned. After Bo and Carly had a symbolic Mayan wedding, everyone headed home.

STEFANO'S BATTLES WITH JOHN AND MARLENA

Stefano's obsession with Marlena and rivalry with John reached new heights in the mid-1990s. His machinations sent the trio on high stakes adventures set in New Orleans, Aremid, and Paris.

New Orleans

In 1994, Stefano held John prisoner in a DiMera family plantation named Maison Blanche. He feared John was remembering too much of his past, so he kept him chained in a dungeon and attempted to brainwash his "pawn" once again. Stefano eventually lured Marlena to Maison Blanche and held her captive as well. In an attempt to stop Stefano from harming John, Marlena tried to seduce Stefano… then drugged his wine before having to go too far. When Kristen decided to hold a charity cotillion at the plantation, Stefano was forced to keep John and Marlena hidden—along with his mystery guest, who turned out to be Hope! Tony, Jennifer, Peter, Bo, and Billie all arrived for the cotillion, unaware of the mansion's secret inhabitants. As a hurricane hit, John and Marlena finally managed to escape with Roman's help. Stefano, meanwhile, was presumed dead.

Aremid

In 1995, Stefano suffered from amnesia after being thrown off a balcony by a possessed Marlena. This new and improved Stefano grew close with his beloved "Queen of the Night," while John found his way back to Kristen. This infuriated Tony, who decided to exact revenge on John. At Peter and Jennifer's wedding in Aremid, Tony framed John for his own murder. Meanwhile, Stefano was struck by lightning and secretly regained his memory. Even though Stefano knew John was innocent, he blackmailed the judge into finding him guilty and had him sentenced to death by the gas chamber. At the last minute, John was saved. Stefano tried to kidnap Marlena by boat but John swam into the ocean and rescued her. Stefano escaped but vowed to return for Marlena.

THE QUEEN OF THE NIGHT

RULE BOOK

Paris

In 1996, Stefano made good on his promise. He kidnapped Marlena and held her in a giant bird cage located in the tunnels beneath Paris. Marlena agreed to sleep with Stefano in exchange for her freedom—however she couldn't go through with it and Stefano flipped out. John tracked them to Paris and set up a masquerade ball to lure out DiMera. The plan backfired, and Stefano captured John and set up a trial with the "people of the night" as the jury. John was found guilty and sentenced to die by guillotine! Marlena rushed to stop it and placed her own head into the contraption just as the blade fell. Stefano stopped the blade in time and tried to kill John again, but Vivian and Ivan came to the rescue. Stefano was once again… presumed dead.

STEPHANIE'S RESCUE

Kayla was wrongly convicted of Marina Toscano's murder. While in prison, she gave birth to Stephanie. Steve hired a nanny named Sheila to help him take care of the baby, but she turned out to be mentally unstable. Sheila was grieving over the loss of her own baby, and soon became obsessed with Stephanie. Sheila eventually kidnapped the child and took off for Australia.

A panicked Kayla escaped from prison, and she and Steve flew to Australia to track down their daughter. They ran into Bo, who had interacted with Sheila without realizing the woman was on the run with his niece. With the help of Marcus Hunter and Grace Jefferies, Steve and Kayla finally caught Sheila in the Australian Outback and were happily reunited with their daughter.

JOHN AND MARLENA'S ITALIAN WEDDING ADVENTURE

In Italy, John led Marlena to a beautiful fountain. Romance was in the air, as he took out a coin, and Marlena made a fervent wish… that they would always be honest with each other. John had more surprises in store for Doc. Romantic music was playing, as John told her wanted to marry her "right here… right now!" The music soared as they kissed. Little did they know, a sinister stranger looked on ominously…

After they tied the knot, the stranger revealed himself as Rico and delivered a message from the DiMeras. He stated that Tony was still in prison, and that Stefano was dead. Rico warned John and Marlena to return to Salem, if they knew what was good for them. John wanted to find out if this is all true. Against Marlena's wishes, he decided to visit the DiMera crypt… if Stefano's body was there, they would go home. However, Stefano's body was not there… he was very much alive!

Jaw-dropping, unexpected wild twists of fate and scandalous secrets:

Susan Hunter Kills David Martin!
- David's daydreams of Julie led to the accidental death of his and Susan's infant son, Dickie.
- Then a grief-stricken Susan shot and killed her negligent husband!

Marie Falls in Love with Her Presumed-dead Brother!
- The Hortons believed eldest son, Tommy Jr., died in the Korean War.
- Then Dr. Mark Brooks came to town and started a romance with Marie. However, Tom soon realized Mark was actually an amnesiac Tommy with plastic surgery.
- The shock of having fallen in love with her brother sent Marie running to the convent!

Addie Dies While Saving Hope!
- Addie and Doug were looking forward to the birth of their child when Addie learned she had leukemia. After giving birth to Hope, she went into remission… only to be struck down by a speeding car while pushing Hope's baby carriage to safety.

Bo Is Victor's Son!
- Bo was about to shoot Victor when Caroline blurted out a long-kept secret—that Victor was his father! The Brady family was stunned to learn Caroline cheated on Shawn with Victor many years ago, resulting in Bo's conception.

The Real Roman Brady Returns!
- As if Marlena's return from the dead wasn't shocking enough, she was soon followed to Salem by the real Roman Brady. It turned out the Roman who had been living in Salem since the mid-1980s was actually John Black, who was brainwashed by Stefano into thinking he was Marlena's husband.

Vivian Buries Carly Alive!
- Thanks to Vivian's special herbs, Dr. Carly Manning was pronounced dead and then buried in the Salem cemetery. In actuality, Carly was still alive and was horrified to wake up six feet under inside her coffin. Vivian taunted her nemesis using a walkie-talkie… but eventually confessed to Lawrence, who dug up his beloved "Katarina."

EJ Wells is Elvis Jr. DiMera!
- Sure, the initials should've been a dead giveaway—but the people of Salem were blindsided to learn EJ Wells was actually Elvis Jr., Stefano's son. Sami was particularly horrified to learn she had been growing close to the son of her family's worst enemy.

Will Is Gay!
- Will Horton had dated Mia McCormick and Gabi Hernandez, so it came as a surprise when Will finally came to terms with his sexuality and announced he was gay. While his grandmother, Marlena, was very supportive, Will's parents, Lucas and Sami, initially had trouble accepting the news. Eventually, both of them came around and reassured their son they loved him more than ever.

Sami Knew about EJ and Abigail's Affair!
- EJ and Abigail thought their secret affair would remain hidden forever. However, after Sami married EJ, she revealed to her husband she had known about his betrayal for months—and she used that time to meticulously plot her revenge!

Additional Shocking Twists Revealed:

Greta's Coronation Ends in a Massacre!	**The Salem Strangler!**
Tom's Secret Passion!	**The Salem Slasher!**
Nicole's Baby Switch!	**The Salem Stalker!**

"By the pricking of my thumbs, something wicked this way comes."

– Stefano DiMera, quoting Shakespeare as he senses something is amiss at Greta's coronation.

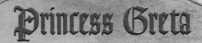

Princess Greta

Once upon a time

…there was a beautiful (though rather muddy) young woman, who lived deep in the swamps of New Orleans. This poor "Swamp Girl" looked quite frightful—until she was given a bath and was revealed to be Greta Von Amberg, the daughter of the wicked Princess Gina Von Amberg.

Once Greta's mother passed away in the year two thousand, Greta was set to inherit the vast Von Amberg fortune and the title of princess. However, Greta had to first prove she was worthy of the crown. Accompanied by her handsome companion, Austin Reed, she endured a series of challenges to test her strength of character in a virtual "Garden of Eden." It was a curious adventure like no other, full of danger and treachery. Yet Greta and Austin, both brave and true of heart, ultimately passed with flying colors.

It was then declared throughout the land that a lavish coronation was to be held to crown the new princess in February, two thousand and one. Citizens of a faraway land called Salem were all in a tizzy—many were excited for their dear friend, while others plotted to use the glamorous ball for their own agendas…

After months of separation, the mischievous yet kindhearted Jack Deveraux desperately wished to be reunited with his beloved Jennifer. Working with Jennifer's wise grandmother, Alice Horton, Jack made plans to crash the party and sweep Jennifer off her feet.

The fair maiden, Belle Black, was excited to attend the coronation, especially since Shawn Brady would also be in attendance. Belle was in love with Shawn but was hesitant to express her feelings since she mistakenly believed he was infatuated with her best friend, Mimi Lockhart.

A conniving witch named Kate Roberts asked her new beau, Vincent Moroni, for an unusual favor—she wanted him to kill her husband, Victor Kiriakis, at the coronation. Moroni was all too eager to grant his lady's request—and added Samantha Brady and Brandon Walker to the list for betraying his daughter, Angela.

Out of love for Samantha, Brandon had married Angela, who was in possession of a priceless recording. It had the power to expose Kate and Lucas' part in the murder of Franco Kelly and their subsequent cover-up. Samantha coveted the recording to use as leverage to regain custody of her son, young William.

So the stage was set for a magical… and perhaps deadly affair. As Salem's finest began their travels to the City of Light, just one question remained: What does one wear to a coronation?

WHAT TO WEAR TO A CORONATION
"My inspiration for the period was Vienna of the 1880s and 1890s, when the waltz became popular. I tried to keep the integrity of the characters. Here they are out of Salem and in a foreign country."

— Richard Bloore, Costume Designer, *Days of our Lives*

On the occasion of the

Coronation of Her Royal Highness Princess Greta

The Comte Von Amberg
is commanded to invite

M. Stefano DiMera

to be present at the
Castle Von Amberg, Paris
on the 12th day of February 2001

Greta's coronation got off to a splendid start as guests arrived in handsome tuxes and exquisite ball gowns. Champagne was flowing, music and laughter filled the air. But all was not right in the City of Light…

When Jennifer discovered Jack in disguise, she was not amused by his antics. She demanded he leave her presence at once!

Belle continued to long for Shawn, who spent much of the evening with a besotted Mimi.

At a late hour, Kate suddenly grew a heart and pleaded with Moroni to halt Victor's execution. Alas, Moroni would not change his mind.

Greta and Austin quietly learned the Von Amberg fortune had actually dried up long ago. However, through the generosity of their guests, they were able to raise an excess of $100 million for orphans in need.

Lastly, a strange creature named Charles lurked in the shadows, glaring at Greta. He was disgruntled over being banished from Castle Von Amberg.

"From this day forward, this young woman will be known throughout the world as Her Royal Highness, the Princess Greta Von Amberg."

— Mrs. Ingrid Mitchell, Von Amberg Chatelaine

Greta was crowned with a beaming Austin by her side. However, the enchanted evening took a deadly turn as Charles raised his gun and fired many shots at the new princess. As everyone ducked for cover, other shots rang out as well…

Moroni's men unleashed several rounds of gunfire on the panicked crowd. Victor was apparently fatally wounded. (Fear not, dear reader—he faked his death!) John, Greta, and Mimi were seriously injured, while Angela died trying to protect Brandon. As her dying wish, Angela demanded her father give the incriminating tape to Brandon and Samantha.

Thus, the coronation came to a terrible end. Soon after, Greta and the rest of the Salem travelers returned home, where they all lived happily ever after. Well… sort of.

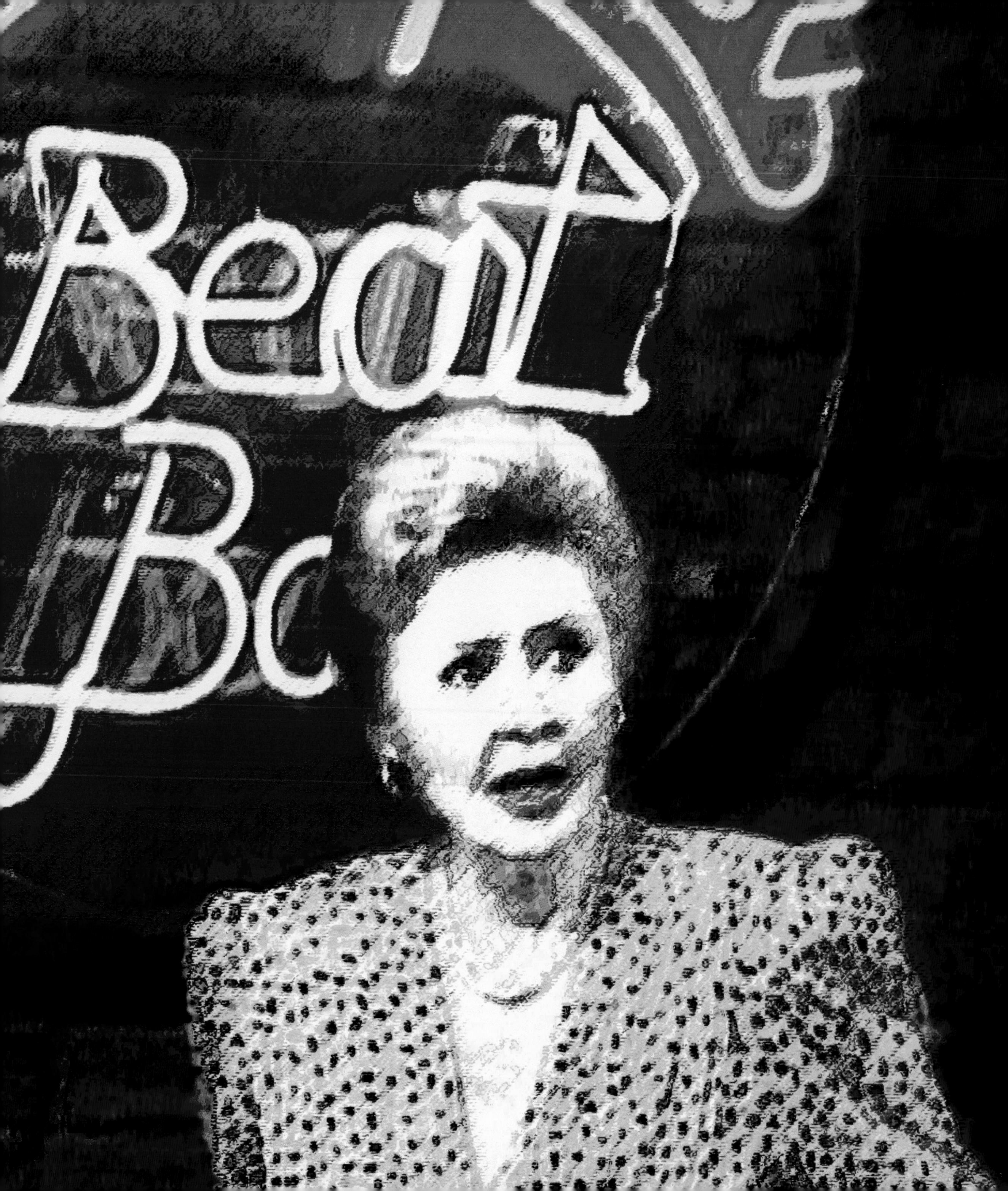
Beat

You can go years
Without realizing
Other people know things
About you
That you don't

You could walk down
The street and
Pass yourself
Without knowing who
It was
You passed

It's hard enough
To catch up
With yourself
And then it doesn't
Do you any good
Because you don't know
Who it is
You've caught up with

The only one
Who really knows
Is the girl
The girl
You first danced with

Keep dancing with me, girl
Don't stop
Please don't stop
If you do
I can't stand
I fall down
I tip over.

Norm de Plume

TOM'S SECRET PASSION

In 1988, Alice was deeply concerned when it became clear Tom was keeping a secret from her. For a while, she even believed he was having an affair with Calliope Jones! What she didn't realize was that Tom was writing and performing beat poetry under the alias Norm de Plume. Determined to uncover the truth, Alice snuck into the Beat Bar… and was stunned to discover Tom reading a poem he wrote about her. She was incredibly moved, and after the performance, Tom came clean.

TOM

Alice, my poetry was the last secret place in my heart you hadn't seen. I was so frightened that, if you didn't like it, if you didn't think it was good, I wouldn't be able to continue to write.

ALICE

I'm deeply flattered that my opinion mattered so much. But, Tom, you know me better than anyone in the world. How could you think I wouldn't be impressed and thrilled with your talent? As of tonight, I'm your biggest fan!

"Baby, Baby… Who's got the baby?"

— story line written by Dena Higley, Co-Head Writer, *Days of our Lives*

It was the winter of 2008. In Salem, USA, Nicole Walker was on top of the world. Forget her sad and tragic past. Forget that her father was a monster who made her a porn star. Forget the tragedy she suffered that made it seemingly impossible for her to carry a baby to term. Things were finally going Nicole's way…

Nicole was living with the man of her dreams, EJ DiMera and she was pregnant with his child.

But Nicole's winning streak abruptly ended when she went into premature labor. Nicole enlisted her ex-lover, Brady Black, to take her to a medical clinic in nearby Brookville. Nicole's baby girl did not survive. A grief-stricken Nicole hatched her plan…

Nicole's To-Do List

1) Blackmail Dr. Baker, the doctor who delivered my premature baby, to pretend I'm still pregnant.
2) Buy and wear a fake pregnancy belly.
3) Lie to EJ, pretend to still be pregnant.
4) Find pregnant teen (Mia) who is willing to give her baby to me.
5) Find out man I love (EJ) has impregnated another woman (Sami).
6) Decide I want EJ's biological baby… the one Sami is secretly carrying. (Sami's pregnancy is so secret, even EJ doesn't know about it.)
7) Lure Sami to Dr. Baker's clinic.
8) Sami has a baby girl.
9) Mia has a baby girl.
10) Talk Dr. Baker into switching babies.
11) Dr. Baker presents Sami with Mia's baby.
12) Lucky for me, I find out that Sami's going to pawn her baby off as a daughter she decided to adopt when she was "out of town" hiding her pregnancy from EJ and the rest of the world.
13) Use Dr. Baker to convince EJ I've just given birth to his daughter. We will name her Sydney. I will raise EJ and Sami's daughter as my own.
14) Marry EJ.

And this plan worked out for Nicole. That is, until Sami's baby, Grace dies. Sami was so traumatized she confessed to EJ that the baby who died was his daughter, which Sami believed to be true. Furious with Sami for lying, he hated her for keeping him from Grace, especially now that it's too late.

Rafe was suspicious of Nicole and ran a DNA test on Nicole's baby. Shock. The baby was really Sami's!

Sami and Nicole had a showdown where Sami slapped the truth out of Nicole. Nicole confessed everything and Sami and EJ were reunited with their biological baby.

THE SALEM STRANGLER

Whodunit: Jake Kositchek. Jake, the younger brother of local entrepreneur Chris Kositchek, was seemingly a nice guy. However, the young man was troubled by the odd behavior of his girlfriend Jessica, which was due to problems related to her childhood. Turns out Jake had even greater issues. He played judge, jury, and executioner to women he felt didn't deserve to live! He called into Dr. Marlena Evans' radio talk show, prompting Det. Roman Brady to camp out on Marlena's floor to protect her.

His victims: Bonnie Bradford, Lori Masters, Denise (a nurse), Mary Anderson, and Samantha Evans (though Jake thought he was killing Marlena!)

Near victims: Renée DuMonde, Marlena Evans, Liz Chandler, and Jessica Blake.

Calling card: Jake left a pink scarf behind after killing his victims. Suspicion fell on Joshua Fallon, who used similar scarves in his self-defense classes.

How He Was Caught: Jake revealed himself to Marlena and planned to kill her, but Roman swooped in to save the day.

Aftermath: Poor Chris was left to wonder what he could have done differently to have prevented his kid brother from slipping to the dark side. With the Salem Strangler behind them, Roman and Marlena looked toward a future—together.

THE SALEM SLASHER

Whodunit: Andre DiMera (Andre disguised himself as Tony and Roman at different times during his reign of terror).

His victims: While Jake's reasons for murder had to do with a deep psychosis, Andre's rational was much simpler—he wanted to do away with anyone who knew that Stefano DiMera was secretly alive. Andre murdered Kelly Chase, Trista Evans Bradford, Jane Doe (a nurse), Leticia Bradford, Daisy, and Renée DuMonde Marshall.

Near victims: Gwen Davies, Hope Williams, Marlena Evans Brady, Marie Horton, and Abigail Abernathy.

Calling card: After stabbing and/or poisoning his victims he left a raven's feather.

How he was caught: Andre's reign of terror seemingly came to an end when he perished in quicksand on Stefano's island in 1984.

Aftermath: Tony mourned his beloved Renée, later finding solace in the arms of his ex-wife, Anna DiMera. Eugene likewise grieved for innocent Trista, and, in time, found a zany soulmate in eccentric Calliope Jones.

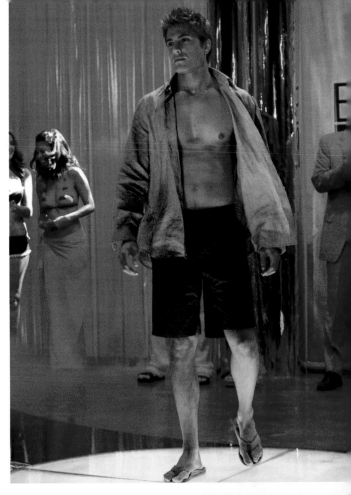

THE SALEM STALKER

On a warm summer evening, many of Salem's residents took part in a splashy Basic Black fashion show. However, the event ended in chaos when the lights went out—and when they came back on, Bo and Hope were found lying in a pool of blood on the runway!

The pair had been hit on the back of their heads with a blunt object and lost a lot of blood. They were rushed to the hospital, where they managed to survive their brutal attack. In the months to come, others would not be so lucky…

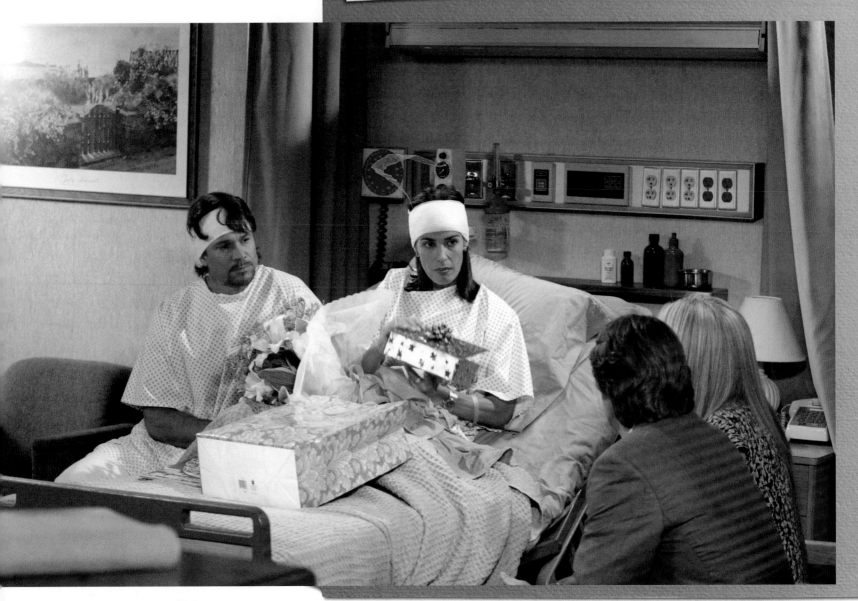

Salem Police Department

INCIDENT /INVESTIGATION REPORT

Officer/ID# Det. John Black (0596)	**Case#** 02-05-003351
	Date/Time Reported 02-18-2005 13:29 Wed
	Last Known Secure 02-18-2005 13:00 Wed
Code 187 – Multiple Homicides	**At Found** 02-18-2005 13:00 Wed

Premise Type Various	**Zone/Tract** Town/5

Location of Incident Various

VICTIMS

#1	Abe Carver	**Weapon/Tools**	Shot at close range – suspect he knew assailant
		MO	
#2	Jack Deveraux	**Weapon/Tools**	blunt force – struck with a brick
		MO	
#3	Maggie Horton	**Weapon/Tools**	blunt force – whiskey bottle
		MO	
#4	Caroline Brady	**Weapon/Tools**	poisoned
		MO	
#5	Cassie DiMera	**Weapon/Tools**	stabbed
		MO	
#6	Roman Brady	**Weapon/Tools**	stabbed
		MO	
#7	Tony DiMera	**Weapon/Tools**	poisoned / injection equipment recovered
		MO	
#8	Doug Williams	**Weapon/Tools**	stabbed
		MO	
#9	Alice Horton	**Weapon/Tools**	force-fed doughnuts / COD – suffocation
		MO	

SUSPECTS

# of Suspect Interviewed		**Crime#** 187	**DOB**	**Sex**	**Relationship To Victims**	**Interviewed by:** J.Black (0596)
#1	**Name (Last First Middle)** Roberts, Lucas	**Crime#**	**DOB**	**Sex**	**Relationship To Victims**	**Interviewed by:**
#2	**Name (Last First Middle)** SEE REVERSE FOR COMPLETE LIST					

CODES: V-Victim (Denote V2, V3)   O=Owner (if other than victim)   R=Reporting Person (if other than victim)

NARRATIVE

Whodunit: Andre DiMera, having survived his death by quicksand in 1984, returned to Salem, determined to ruin the lives of many families by going on a murder spree. Andre repeated his method of operations when he wore a latex mask to pretend to be Roman when he was the Slasher, only this time Andre used unique treachery to make Marlena think that she was the killer.

RIP: Victor Kiriakis was nearly killed during this time, too, but by Jan Spears who electrocuted Victor in his bathtub. (It was mistakenly believed by some that Victor had been done in by the Stalker.)

Weapon of Choice: The killer used a variety of items to do away with his victims. Maggie, an alcoholic, was cruelly clubbed to death with a bottle of whiskey. Meanwhile, "Marlena" did in poor Alice by stuffing donuts down her throat until she couldn't breathe. Later, "Marlena" cruelly joked that she did away with Alice before getting her donut recipe!

Near Victims: Marlena, Kate, Sami, Bonnie, Mimi, Belle, Celeste

How he was caught: Andre's victims (and Victor) weren't buried in graves but rather transported to Melaswen, a secret island that had a section that was an exact duplicate of Salem. In time, they were rescued and made their way back to their loved ones. Someone asked how could so many people truly be alive? "A DiMera hoax" was offered up as the reason. "What else?" an exasperated Julie added!

Reporting Officer/ID# 0596	**Supervisor:** R Brady	**Page** 1
Dept. Homocide	**Case Disposition:** Closed	
Status **Signature**	**Case Status:** Closed	02/23/2005 16:49:24

Printed by SPD5462, XSP0597

Sys#: 97768

235

Abe is shot and misses Theo's christening.

Celeste began having premonitions foretelling Abe's death. Abe was frightened when Tom Horton's ghost whispered his name—according to Alice, it meant he was doomed. Lexie made Abe promise he would retire early from the police force, and they took precautions to keep him safe.

On the day of Theo's christening, the Carvers' friends and family gathered at St. Luke's. Per Celeste's latest vision, Lexie warned Abe to stay home until noon. Just as the clock began to chime, Abe stepped outside his house—and was immediately shot!

Abe fought to hang on and managed to indicate he knew the culprit. Unfortunately, he died before he could name his killer.

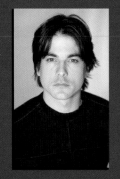

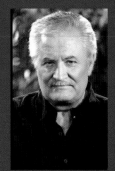

Lucas   Sami   Rex   Nicole   Victor   Tony   Kate

The "Salem Seven" Suspects

The suspects in Abe's murder became known as the Salem Seven.

NO ONE IS SAFE.

Like sands through
the hourglass...
this is the nightmare
of their lives.

Days of our Lives
The Salem Stalker

CORDAY PRODUCTIONS INC. presents DAYS OF OUR LIVES: THE SALEM STALKER KRISTIAN ALFONSO KYLE BRANDT TANYA BOYD JOHN CLARKE JASON COOK JUDI EVANS FARAH FATH PETER RECKELL SUZANNE ROGERS ALEXIS THORPE
Music Composed by KEN CORDAY and D. BRENT NELSON Production Designer DAN OLEXIEWICZ Costume Designer RICHARD BLOORE Editors G. MASON DIXON LUIGI POWERS DAVID MAWHINNEY SCHOONER DARROW
Senior Coordinating Producers JANET SPELLMAN RIDER TOM WALKER Consulting Producer JAMES E. REILLY Producer ROY G. STEINBERG Co-Executive Producer STEPHEN WYMAN Executive Producer KEN CORDAY Headwriter JAMES E. REILLY
Written by VICTOR GIALANELLA PETER BRASH RICK DRAUGHON JEANNE MARIE GRUNWELL RENEE GODELIA FRAN MYERS and SOFIA LANDON GEIER (Part I) and JODIE SCHOLZ (Part II) Directed by STEPHEN WYMAN (Part I) and PHIL SOGARD (Part II)
©2003 Corday Productions Inc. Distributed by Sony Pictures Television

 NBC NOVEMBER 4 & 5

Jack investigated his friend's death, determined to solve the murder. Jennifer worried he was risking his life, and her fears proved valid when Jack was bludgeoned with a brick in an alley behind Salem Place. Jack died soon after at the hospital.

Under hypnosis with Marlena, Maggie remembered she witnessed Abe's murder. However, she was unable to recall the identity of the killer.

On Halloween night, Mickey and Maggie stayed home to keep her safe. Unable to sleep, Maggie went down to the kitchen, where there was a knock at the door. Recognizing her guest, she invited the person inside. As they shared a cup of tea, Maggie soon realized she was staring into the eyes of the killer. She was then viciously struck with a bottle of alcohol (a cruel irony given her past as an alcoholic).

At the police station, Hope, Bo, Shawn, Mimi, Cassie, and Philip watched a delayed feed coming from Mickey and Maggie's house. They were horrified when an image of Maggie's bloodied body appeared on screen. Maggie later succumbed to her injuries before she could reveal the person responsible.

Family and friends gathered at a memorial for Abe, Jack, and Maggie. During the service, Bo received a message from the killer that Caroline would be the next to die and her murder would take place within the hour. The threat was punctuated with the arrival of a fourth coffin—with Caroline's name on it. Though initially panicked, everyone was relieved when time ran out and Caroline was still alive.

Before going home, Caroline wanted to pray in the chapel. Assuming no one could get past them, Bo and the rest of the Bradys waited in the vestibule, believing Caroline would be safe. Bo was horrified when he later found his mother dead inside the chapel—the victim of poisoning.

FALL FESTIVAL DAYS/ PARADE

Piñata Party & Prizes

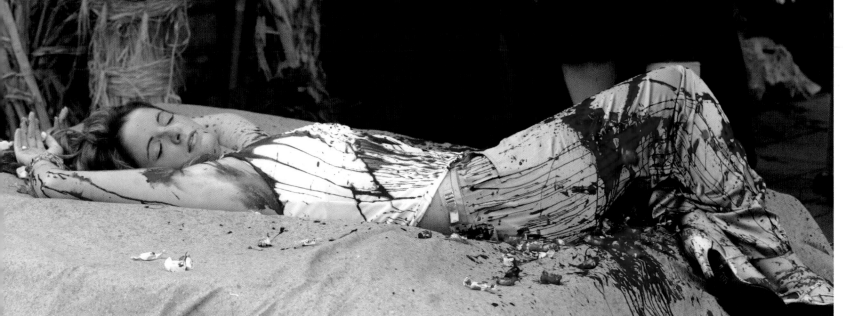

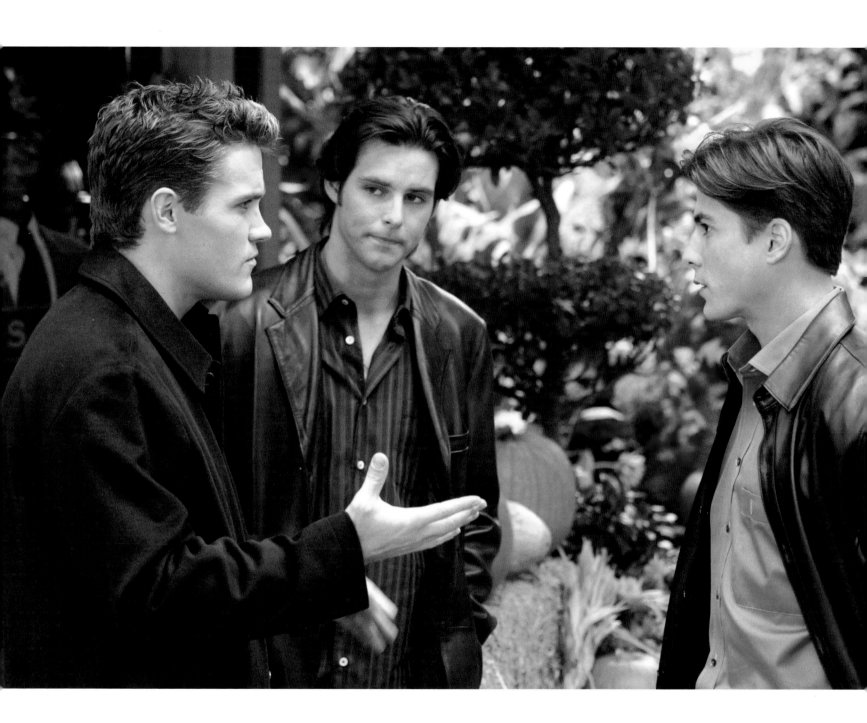

Celeste continued to have visions of the deceased warning her of more murders to come. Meanwhile, Cassie figured out the identity of the Salem Stalker. After receiving a call from the killer, she rushed out to tell the police. However, poor Cassie would not get very far…

At Salem Place, the children of Salem got a nasty surprise when they broke open a turkey piñata—and Cassie's bloody body came tumbling out!

BONNIE'S
CHRISTMAS TREES
All Proceeds Donated to Charity

Mimi's mom, Bonnie, opened a Christmas Tree lot during the holidays. During her downtime, Bonnie plotted to snatch herself a wealthy widow in Mickey—and fantasized about seducing him.

Unmoved by the holiday spirit, the Salem Stalker made an appearance at the Christmas Tree lot and terrorized Sami, Bonnie, Mimi, and Bonnie's dog, Max. Roman, Rex, and Shawn came to the rescue but the killer got away.

★ ★ ★ SALEM ★ ★ ★

SPECTATOR

PUBLISHED DAILY

LATEST NEWS

Vol. CXDV, No. 50,333

Largest Circulation In Our History

50 CENTS

POLICE COMMANDER ABE CARVER SLAIN

★ ★ ★ SALEM ★ ★ ★

SPECTATOR

PUBLISHED DAILY

Maggie Horton B Murdered on Hal

By Sherry Kaufman
Staff Reporter

THE INTRUDER

2004
ISSUE 872
VOL. LCXVXII

WILL PSYCHIC LEAD POLICE TO KILLER?

★ ★ ★ SALEM ★ ★ ★

SPECTATOR

PUBLISHED DAILY

LATEST NEWS

Vol. CXDV, No. 50,333

Serial Killer Strike Who's

★ ★ ★ SALEM ★ ★ ★

SPECTATOR

PUBLISHED DAILY

LATEST NEWS

Vol. CXDV, No. 50,333

Largest Circulation In Our History

50 CENTS

Caroline Brady Poisoned

4th Death Linked to Serial Slayer

By Ralph Hernandez, Jr.
Staff Reporter

regarding the sit-
main the same, state
orities. Details con-
ne action have been
eliminary investiga-
t is felt that only by
etailed study will the
s become known.
at this conference all
ernments found them-
n unanimous agree-
garding this undertak-
ngements for dealing
ions and

Many persons feel at this
stage that some legal action is

Future plans will, of neces-
sity, have great bearing on the

Many pers
stage that son
forthcoming
comes commo
there is press
side which
change the a
Of no less
the comm
shown of t
menace fro
peace of o
cerns all o
properly is
sultation
This wa
strum

Despite the constant threat of danger, the people of Salem were determined to celebrate the holiday season. Belle finally returned from a month-long visit to Europe, where her family and Shawn had sent her to keep her out of harm's way. She and Shawn reunited just in time for Christmas.

As the year drew to a close, many people hoped the horrors of the past few months might finally have come to an end. The town was full of good cheer as everyone looked forward to a new year and perhaps a new beginning. And what better way to start things off than the joyous occasion of Roman and Kate's New Year's Eve wedding…

On New Year's Eve, Roman and Kate finally tied the knot. During the reception at Tuscany, guests were horrified when the newlyweds cut their wedding cake—and it oozed "blood." While Celeste was upset by yet another premonition of death, Alice took charge and provided her famous donuts to replace the cake and everything seemed back on track…

Roman walked into the kitchen and came face-to-face with the killer. Kate went looking for her husband, and at midnight, she stunned all the wedding guests by emerging from the kitchen covered in blood. Having found her husband stabbed to death, she let out an anguished scream.

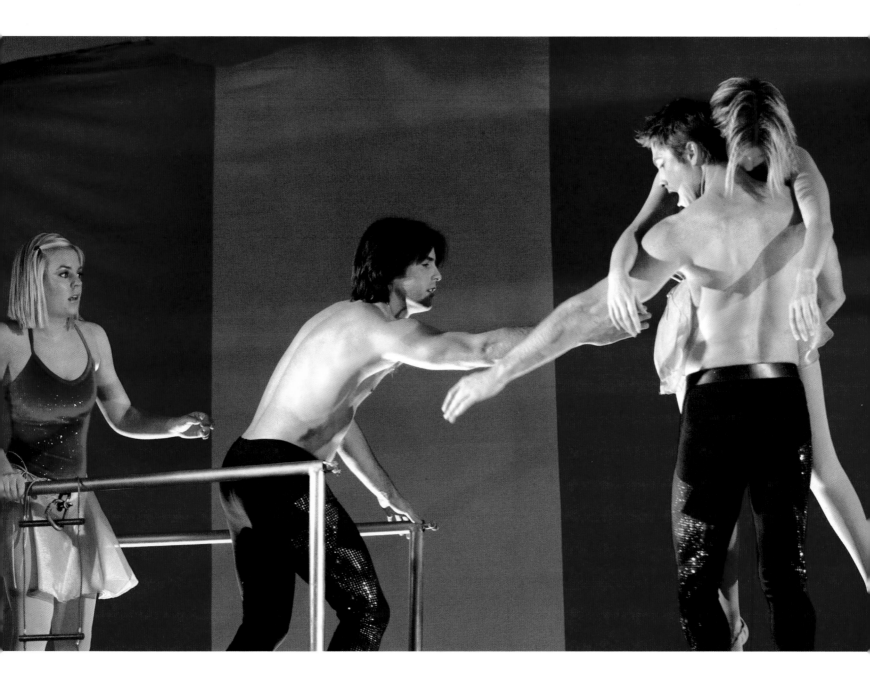

Amidst all the tragedy, the Horton Foundation hosted a charity circus event. Doug and Julie returned to town with a Bengal tiger to perform in the show.

The day of the fundraiser, Salem residents woke up to an anonymous ad in the newspaper announcing that the identity of the serial killer will be revealed at the circus!

At the event, the Hortons surprised Alice with a birthday cake and a touching tribute. Then the show began with Mickey acting as ringmaster. Philip, Shawn, Rex, Mimi, and Belle dazzled the crowd with a high-wire act—which went awry when Mimi fainted midperformance. The guys pulled off a daring rescue.

When Sami heard Lucas was planning a knife-throwing act with Kate, she decided to use it to her advantage. She locked Lucas in a portable restroom, and took his place. Blaming Kate for her father's death, Sami began throwing real knives at her! Lucas managed to escape and prevented Sami from harming his mother. Sami swore she just wanted to scare Kate (um, right).

Bedlam erupted as everyone ran for safety. John and Shawn managed to distract the animal when it cornered Belle, though it ended up attacking John when the tranquilizer gun jammed. Shawn managed to scare off the tiger so John only suffered minor injuries.

Meanwhile the tent was plunged into darkness as the killer disabled the lights. By the time the emergency lights came on, the tiger had dragged Tony away and the hunt was on… for Tony, the tiger, and the killer.

Tony, severely mauled by the tiger, was found and rushed to the hospital.

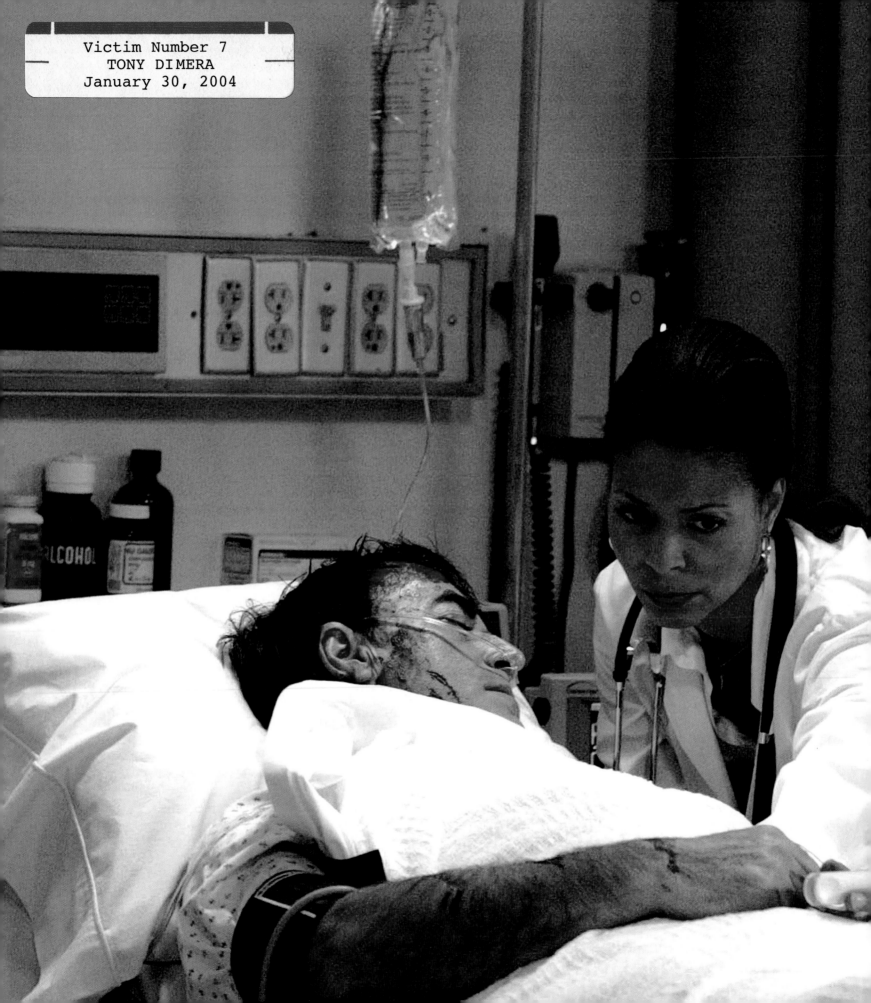

In order to stop Tony from speaking, the killer went into his hospital room and prepared to inject Tony with a deadly drug. Tony opened his eyes and confronted the Salem Stalker—who was revealed to be Marlena! "I knew it was you," he whispered as a deadly Marlena administered the drug. Tony went into cardiac arrest and died, taking the secret with him.

Doug figured out Marlena was the killer. Without revealing what he suspected, Doug consulted Celeste, who put him in touch with the spirit world. After getting the confirmation he needed, he visited the cemetery to speak to Addie's grave. Marlena came upon him, and a confrontation ensued. Marlena stabbed him with a letter opener, and though seriously injured, Doug managed to scramble away. While hiding, he wrote Marlena's name in blood on a piece of paper before collapsing. Bo and Hope found him but it was too late—Doug's life slipped away.

Alice eventually found Doug's note, and Marlena arrived at the Horton house with a letter opener, itching to kill again. Marlena demanded the note but Alice refused to give it to her. Alice pleaded with Marlena to put a stop to the madness… but to no avail.

When Bo and Hope arrived at the house, they found Alice barely alive, surrounded by her famous donuts. Alice then passed away, having suffocated from a donut fragment that had been stuffed in her throat.

Alice's shocking death was the final murder of the Salem Stalker.

By this time, John had figured out Marlena was the killer. Though he didn't want to believe his beloved Doc was capable of such evil, he confronted her. Marlena confessed—but she wasn't giving up without a fight. They struggled on the balcony of her penthouse, and Marlena accidentally fell to the ground below.

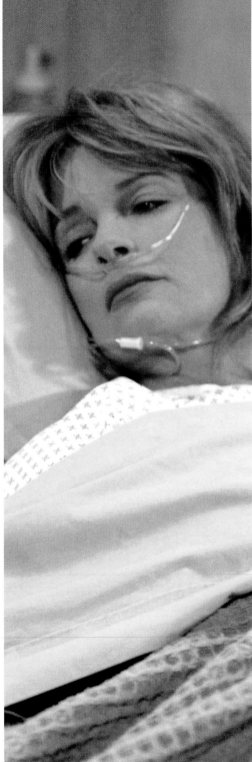

At the hospital, Marlena claimed she had no idea why she confessed and swore she was innocent. John realized there could be another explanation—and stunned everyone by tracking down Hattie Adams. However, Marlena's look-alike had an airtight alibi.

Marlena finally agreed to take truth serum. While under the influence of the drug, Marlena confessed to all the killings! She explained she had committed murder because she was still in love with Roman. She had wanted to break up her ex-husband and Kate, and when Abe found out, she got rid of him. Everyone else was killed because they eventually knew too much.

Marlena went to prison for her crimes. However, she was later shot and killed during a staged prison break.

On the day of her funeral, Marlena woke up inside her coffin and realized she was about to be buried alive! She clawed at her casket and cried for help. Eventually, she passed out, and when she woke up again, she was on a strange island made to look exactly like Salem. Marlena wandered around "Salem Place," and to her stunned amazement, Marlena ran into Alice Horton!

Marlena sat next to Alice and assumed she had joined her in the afterlife. Alice gently corrected her. "You're not dead, you're alive. I'm alive, we're very much alive!"

Marlena was soon reunited with her "victims," who explained she hadn't killed anyone. It was all some elaborate hoax. Though Marlena was relieved she was not a murderer, it soon became clear their nightmare was not yet over as she and the others were being held prisoner on the island.

Months later, Tony revealed he had been behind the entire thing. He wanted to get back at everyone who had wronged him. In particular, he still held a grudge against John for stealing Kristen from him, and he was also jealous that Stefano favored John as his loyal solider. Eventually all the hostages managed to escape the island and return home. Years later, it was revealed "Tony" was actually Andre DiMera.

Double your pleasure, double your fun? Not always! Certainly not in the case of these doppelgangers who inhabited the town of Salem! Imagine, your look-alike infiltrating your life and wreaking havoc, or better yet, sleeping with your spouse? These "doubles" and their masterminds certainly came up with some innovative ways for these characters to be stand-ins! From Andre and Tony DiMera, Rafe Hernandez and Arnold Feniger, Marlena Evans and Hattie Adams, Marlena Evans and Samantha Evans, Hope Williams Brady and Princess Gina Von Amberg, and Kristen DiMera and Susan Banks… these dead-ringers pulled the wool over unsuspecting people's eyes in the most elaborate of ways!

- **Marlena and Samantha Evans**—Dr. Marlena Evans was a psychiatrist at Bayview Sanitarium. However, her jealous twin sister wanted the life Marlena had. So, she drugged the good doctor, and admitted her to Bayview as a patient while Samantha impersonated her. Samantha, as Marlena, even ordered shock treatments to keep her sister locked away. Eventually, her plot came to light, and Samantha was arrested. Samantha was played by Deidre Hall's real-life twin sister, Andrea Gengler.

- **Andre and Tony DiMera**—Andre, while impersonating Tony, would perpetrate dastardly and destructive acts on his enemies: framing John Black for murder, orchestrating the Sami and Stan plot, and being the brains behind the Salem Stalker plot, among many.

- **Kristen DiMera and Susan Banks**—Kristen became obsessed with holding on to the man she loves, John Black. Enter Susan Banks, who Stefano paid to impersonate his daughter through a makeover that made her look exactly like Kristen. Susan got pregnant via Stefano, and was to give up her baby to Kristen to pass off as Kristen's child with John, only things went awry.

- **Hope Williams and Princess Gina**—Princess Gina Von Amberg was an accomplished art thief instrumental in Stefano DiMera's plots, but she went MIA. So, Stefano brainwashed Hope to take her place, since they looked almost identical! Gina eventually had surgery to look exactly like Hope and headed to Salem to reunite with her former lover, John Black. But, Gina ended up kidnapping Hope and taking her place, and almost married Bo!

- **Marlena and Hattie Adams**—In his vendetta against Marlena, Stefano DiMera found a woman named Hattie Adams who bore a slight resemblance to her. Under the skillful hands of Dr. Rolf, Hattie had plastic surgery to increase this resemblance. Hattie eventually became obsessed and went even further with this plot to look identical to Marlena. Hattie was yet another role played by Deidre Hall's real-life twin sister, Andrea.

- **Rafe and Arnold Feniger**—In an attempt by Stefano and EJ DiMera to destroy Sami and Rafe's marriage, they hired an out-of-work actor who answered their casting ad. The actor, Arnold, would become Rafe through plastic surgery, while Stefano kidnapped, brainwashed, and locked up the real Rafe in an institution. Faux Rafe was actually a sleazy crook who hated Sami's children, and even murdered Nicole's mother, Fay Walker, in the process of this switch.

Seeing Double

THE BANKS QUADRUPLETS

Susan Banks

Kindhearted, gullible, and quirky—and she loves her some Elvis Presley! She even named her son after the King. Though that mean, mean, mean Kristen often pulled the wool over her eyes, Susan managed to thwart her nemesis in the end.

Sister Mary Moira

One of the Banks quadruplets. She's a harsh, no-nonsense nun, who had no problem going toe-to-toe with the diabolical Kristen in order to defend her sister.

Thomas Banks

Susan and Sister Mary Moira's shady gangster brother. Susan sought his help to steal back baby Elvis from Kristen. However, Sister Mary Moira quickly put a stop to that.

Penelope Kent

The long-lost member of the Banks quadruplets. She's a glamorous British actress, who was given up for adoption by Susan's mother because she couldn't afford to raise four children. Penelope tracked down Susan when she saw her picture in the paper—but was soon killed by Edmund, who mistook her for Kristen.

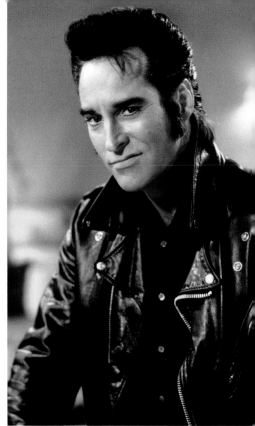

SUSAN'S STORY

(You're the) Devil in Disguise

- In 1996, Kristen was desperate to hang on to John. When she miscarried their baby, she kept it a secret, fearing John would leave her for Marlena. Her father, Stefano, came up with a solution to her problem in the form of a pregnant, Elvis Presley-loving woman named Susan Banks. When donning a blond wig and false teeth, Susan looked surprisingly just like Kristen—although the two women could not be less alike. While Kristen was sophisticated and cunning, Susan was eccentric and naïve. However, with a little coaching, Susan was able to impersonate Kristen, and she promised to give up her baby once it was born so Kristen could pass it off as her own.

Can't Help Falling In Love

- While posing as Kristen, Susan gave birth to John, Jr. in February of 1997. John married "Kristen" right before the birth, but of course it wasn't valid. Kristen insisted Susan's job was done but Susan grew attached to her baby—and to John! Unable to get rid of her, Kristen was forced to hire kooky Susan as the baby's nanny. Realizing Ms. Banks was becoming a problem, Stefano built a secret room in the mansion where Susan could be imprisoned.

Suspicious Minds

- Marlena befriended Susan and soon figured out Kristen's devious plot. Marlena confronted Kristen, who then locked Marlena in the secret room! Susan realized what happened to her new friend, but once she learned Marlena also loved John, she figured it was best to keep her in the room. Susan managed to lock Kristen in with Marlena, and the two rivals had a knockdown, drag-out fight. Susan proceeded to take over Kristen's life. Watching a TV monitor, Marlena and Kristen were horrified to see Susan seduce an unwitting John.

All Shook Up

- Susan convinced John to renew their vows in what turned out to be an Elvis-themed ceremony. Laura Horton crashed the wedding and accused "Kristen" of kidnapping Marlena. Laura shook Susan so hard that her fake teeth went flying through the air and landed in Vivian's martini glass! Exposed, Susan was forced to make a full confession, and John raced down to the secret room to save Kristen and Marlena, who had passed out from a gas leak. John denounced Kristen for her lies, and he and Marlena married a month later. Meanwhile, Susan gained custody of her son and renamed him Elvis Jr. (EJ).

SUSAN AND EDMUND'S COURTSHIP

John and Marlena sent Susan and baby Elvis to England to escape from Stefano and Kristen. While hiding out, Susan was befriended by Violet, the proprietor of the local pub. Susan was hit by Cupid's arrow when she met Violet's son, Edmund Phineas Crumb. The two bonded over their love for Elvis Presley and soon realized they were kindred souls. Edmund and Susan spent the next few weeks getting to know each other while playing darts and riding out into the English countryside. Before getting their "happily ever after," they had to contend with a conniving Kristen, but eventually the quirky pair got married in Bermuda and returned to England to raise Elvis, Jr.

THE REIGN OF PRINCESS GINA

During the four years that Hope was presumed dead, Stefano had implanted into her mind the memories of Princess Gina, an art thief who painted over masterpieces. In 1999, The Phoenix transformed Hope back into Gina in order to reclaim his art pieces from Vivian Alamain.

Under Stefano's influence Hope kidnapped John and turned him evil. The two made love on a submarine after John went missing during a swim on his honeymoon with Marlena. Next, Stefano and Hope (as Gina) made love. Soon, the real Princess Gina was revealed to be alive. She'd been living in a castle waiting for John to come back to her. Eventually, Hope was able to fight off the Gina persona and regained her true personality. Trouble loomed ahead as Gina lured Hope to her castle and held both her and Stefano as prisoners. Meanwhile, impersonating Hope, Gina goes to Salem where she eventually raises suspicions from both Bo and Shawn.

Fearing her ruse has been discovered and is about to be revealed, she forces Shawn at gunpoint to jump off a ledge. He falls only a short distance landing on another terrace. Gina then tries to force Marlena to do the same. As Bo wrestles with Gina, the gun accidentally shoots her in the struggle. On her deathbed, Gina reveals to her daughter Greta the true identity of her father.

Bo, convinced that "Hope" has perished, is devastated. At the funeral the casket falls open revealing a scar on "Hope's" body, which Lili Faversham recognizes as belonging to Gina. Bo immediately begins to search for the real Hope. Shortly thereafter, he and John rescue Hope and Stefano from the castle.

Tears, anguish, death, and heartbreak are commonplace in the world of daytime drama, but when a story moves its audience, and makes them feel what their favorite characters are feeling, you've struck gold. From long-awaited reunions, to grief-stricken parents coping with the loss of a child, to saying good-bye to a beloved family member, or standing by helplessly watching someone die of a terminal illness—each of these story lines guarantees one thing—a good cry.

- **Hope pleads for her life as she is suspended in a cage over a vat of acid**—After being kidnapped by Ernesto Toscano and taken to a cave, Hope is held captive over a vat of acid, while her beloved Bo watches in horror. Hope, in tears, has to say her final good-byes to Bo. In a harrowing moment, a helpless Bo watches as the cage explodes over the vat of acid, and Hope is presumed dead.

- **Marlena and Roman reunite on the pier**—After "dying" in a plane crash, Marlena spent almost four years in a coma. When she was finally able to get back to Salem to be reunited with her husband, "Roman Brady" (who later would turn out to be John Black), she did it in the most heart-stopping way! On the Salem pier (a spot that has always been magical for their relationship) out of the fog, Roman saw a figure. Marlena walked slowly towards Roman and said, "Roman!… It's Marlena!" With tears streaming down her face, and tears streaming down his, the couple embraced, kissed, and held each other as more tears flowed. The performances by Deidre Hall (Marlena) and Drake Hogestyn (John) were mesmerizing, many Kleenex boxes around the country were worn out!

- **Isabella dies in John's arms**—Isabella Toscano was diagnosed with pancreatic cancer. With not long to live, she asked the love of her life, John Black, to take her to her real home in Venice, Italy. Along with their infant son, Brady, they made this final trip. Isabella's condition deteriorated rapidly. After saying goodnight to her son one last time, she asked John to dance with her. Wanting to grant his wife's dying wish, John picked up Isabella in his arms and swayed to the music playing in the background. He imagined dancing with a healthy Isabella. Then John was snapped back to reality when he realized Isabella was dead, and began to sob uncontrollably.

- **Hope is grief-stricken after Zack is killed in a hit and run accident**—In one of *Days of our Lives* most tragic story lines, Bo and Hope were forced to do the unthinkable… say good-bye to their three-year-old son Zack, who was hit by a car. In a horrific turn of events Bo's daughter Chelsea asked her father if she could borrow his car, even though she hadn't gotten her driver's license yet. He agreed. While using her cell phone and pumping up the music in the car, Chelsea did not see that her half-brother Zack had walked into the street. She hit him with the car. Hope happened upon the scene and was beside herself. Once at Universal Hospital, Dr. Lexie Carver had to deliver the bad news that Zack was brain dead and on life support. Eventually, Bo and Hope had to let the boy go, crushing Hope forever, and putting a huge wedge in Bo and Hope's marriage. Kristian Alfonso delivered a powerful performance in a story about a mother's worst nightmare.

- **Daniel informs Sami that baby Grace is going to die**—Sami, who believes Grace is her biological daughter, (only it is Mia's baby, thanks to a baby-switch via Nicole) is grief-stricken when baby Grace comes down with bacterial meningitis. Dr. Daniel Jonas informs Sami and Rafe that the baby is not going to make it, and the couple decides to sit at the little girl's bedside when she dies. Sami later revealed to EJ that he was "Grace's biological father," still unaware that the baby she had raised was not theirs at all.

- **Alice's memorial**—In one of the most sorrowful, touching, and tearful episodes, *Days of our Lives* eulogized Alice Horton after her passing, and that of her portrayer (original cast member and matriarch, Frances Reid). In a moving gathering, Hope, Jennifer, Bo, and the Horton family and loved ones, each said some heartfelt words about the incredible woman that influenced each of their lives. While Alice was no longer living, she lives on through them for the rest of the days of their lives.

- **Lexie dies**—Dr. Lexie Carver had an inoperable brain tumor. She revealed to her family that she did not have long to live. Finally, sitting with her husband, Abe, outside their home and watching night fall, Lexie passed away, and Abe broke down while cradling Lexie in his arms.

EJ'S MURDER

In 2014, Sami and EJ had been estranged for months after she learned of his affair with Abigail Deveraux. EJ never wavered in his desire to work things out, but a scorned Sami kept pushing him away. Finally, Sami could no longer deny she was still deeply in love with her husband, and the two reunited, privately renewing their wedding vows in their living room. However, their happiness would not last long.

Sami's entire world was turned upside down when EJ was suddenly shot and killed during an argument with Clyde Weston. Sami found EJ lying in a pool of blood in the park. As she tearfully begged him not to leave her, EJ managed to utter, "I love you, Samantha" one last time before slipping away. Sami went into a state of shock and denial. After saying a haunting good-bye to EJ in the morgue, Sami went home and had to break the news to Johnny, Allie, and Sydney. Soon after, Sami and the kids moved to Los Angeles to start their life over.

THE LOVE STORY OF MICKEY AND MAGGIE

Mickey Horton had a heart attack, and then suffered a stroke that left him an amnesiac after a confrontation with his "son" Mike over his affair with Linda Anderson. An upset Mickey sneaked away from University Hospital and wandered to the small farm town of Brookville. There he met Maggie, a young woman who was in an auto accident that killed her parents and left her crippled. Maggie had never had a man look her in the eyes, and ignore her crutches—but this stranger did. She fell in love with this man who treated her like a woman for the first time, but boy, was it complicated… very complicated! It became one of *Days of our Lives*, greatest and most dramatic stories, involving Laura, Bill, Mike, Mickey, and Maggie…

"It was always so gut-wrenching that Tom could see that Mickey loved Maggie, and Tom knew that Bill and Laura were getting closer. It was really the twists and turns of the story that were so incredible. It gave Bill, Laura, Mickey and Maggie, Tom and Alice, all these things to think about… and worry about."

— Suzanne Rogers, Maggie Simmons

THE EVENTS:

- Mickey shows up at Maggie's door, and asks for a glass of water after breaking out of the hospital in the small town of Brookville.

- Suffering from amnesia, Mickey looks at his belt buckle, seeing the initials "M.H." he tells Maggie his name is "Marty Hansen". He had no memory of being Mickey Horton.

- With "Marty's" encouragement Maggie goes to Salem University Hospital for a consultation with Dr. Laura Horton. Maggie is shocked when she sees a wedding picture of Laura and Mickey in the doctor's office.

- Feeling inferior, Maggie rushes out—afraid that Mickey will leave her if he realizes that he is married to this beautiful woman and successful doctor.

- Brookville County Fair: photos were taken with Maggie, Marty, and their friends Hank and Jay. Dr. Tom Horton sees the photo in the newspaper and realizes it's his missing son, Mickey!

- Arriving at the farm in Brookville, Tom identifies himself to Mickey who doesn't know who he is.

- When "Marty" leaves the room, Maggie pleads with Tom not to tell "Marty" that he is Mickey Horton and take him back to Salem.

- Tom leaves but later returns with Laura and Bill who bring photos of Mickey. After looking at the photos, he chooses to stay with Maggie.

- Maggie is convinced to have back surgery to help her walk without crutches. Dr. Bill Horton performs the operation but she still doesn't walk. He informs Mickey that the operation was a success, and there is no reason Maggie shouldn't be walking!

- If she returns "normal," Maggie thinks Mickey will leave her for Laura. Mickey surprises her with a pair of red shoes, saying he would like to take her dancing.

- At physical therapy Maggie meets another patient, a football player, who takes an interest in her. Mickey gets jealous which forces Maggie to confess she is jealous of his wife, Laura.

- Maggie is inspired to walk again. She puts on the red dancing shoes and she and Mickey dance.

- Mickey finds out that Mike Horton is not his biological son when Mike comes to visit his dad at the farm. While Mike is helping Mickey do the chores, he gets injured and is taken to the hospital and he needs a blood transfusion. Mickey is prepared to give blood, but his blood does not match.

- Mickey asks Laura if her blood matches… it doesn't, and she has to reveal that Bill is Mike's father, not Mickey, causing him to remember everything! Mickey goes on a rampage and shoots Bill in the hand. Mickey is confined to a sanitarium.

THE DEATH OF ZACK

A devastating tragedy struck the Brady family on New Year's Eve.

Bo had recently discovered trouble-making Chelsea was his daughter, and he was trying to do everything he could to be a father to her. On that fateful night, Chelsea talked Bo into letting her borrow his car even though she didn't have a license. While driving, she got distracted and hit something—not realizing it was her little brother, Zack.

When Hope went to pick up Zack at his sleepover, she found her son's slipper out on the street. Hope then discovered her son's lifeless body and cried out in deep anguish.

Hope and Bo waited anxiously at the hospital as Lexie worked feverishly to save the boy she once raised as her own. To everyone's horror, little Zack didn't make it.

The grief-stricken parents said an emotional and painful good-bye to their son. Soon after, they were hit with another terrible blow—the car responsible for running over Zack belonged to Bo! An angry Bo quickly took Chelsea aside. Completely devastated by the news, Chelsea insisted she had no idea she hit Zack—and she begged her father not to tell Hope the truth! Chlesea's mom, Billie, quickly learned what happened, and she made the stunning decision to take the blame.

A distraught Hope ripped into Billie. Bo wanted to tell the truth but realized he needed to be there for Hope and help her through her despair. This proved to be a monumental mistake because when the truth finally came out, Hope was livid that Bo kept such a huge secret from her. In her grief and anger, she blamed her husband for Zack's death, and the two separated. For a while it looked like their relationship was over for good, but eventually, their deep love for one another brought them back together—and they welcomed another child, Ciara, into the world.

THE DEATH OF MADISON JAMES

A series of underground explosions literally rocked Salem to its core. Among the many casualties were Jack Deveraux and Madison James. Madison was set to marry Brady that night, but she died in the arms of her estranged ex-husband, Ian McAllister. Ian declared his love for Madison, but her last thoughts were of Brady. Ian's lover, Kate, stewed as she learned of his true feelings.

THE DEATH OF LEXIE CARVER

Lexie was dealt devastating news—she had an inoperable brain tumor. She bravely made the choice to forgo treatment of any kind and instead decided to live out the rest of her days on her own terms. She began checking things off her "bucket list" and spent quality time with her family and friends. She also filmed home videos for Theo to watch as he grew older. In the end, Lexie died peacefully in Abe's arms as they admired their beautiful garden.

"DOOL"
ISABELLA.
STACI
WEDDING
9 MONTHS PREG.

BLOORE
'92

ISABELLA'S DEATH

John Black and Isabella Toscano were about to get married in a beautiful ceremony at St. Luke's. However, as they recited their vows, a pregnant Isabella suddenly went into labor! She gave birth to their son, Brady, and then the glowing couple completed their vows in front of their family, friends, and newborn baby.

Their happiness, however, was short-lived. A few months later, Isabella was diagnosed with pancreatic cancer. John and Isabella travelled to Venice, where she lived out her last moments. As she started to slip away, Isabella dreamt of sharing one last dance with John… and then she peacefully died in his arms.

In the following years, Isabella made many ghostly appearances to John and Brady, often to provide comfort or words of advice.

TRIBUTE TO ALICE HORTON

The town united for a beautiful and touching funeral service in which they share their favorite memories and kind words about Alice.

While there is plenty of drama and intrigue in the town of Salem, there is also time for citizens to let their hair down, have some fun, show their hidden talents, and enjoy life. Amidst all the tears there is laughter too! *Days of our Lives* has had some rather unusual and whimsical marriages, celebrations, and even love affairs that have made the characters on the canvas endearing to fans of the show, and become even more dimensional. Comedic relief can often be the order of the day that puts a smile on the television audience's faces, and a smile on the cast who often get to take a short time-out from all their character's troubles.

- **Calliope Jones and Eugene Bradford love story**—
Eugene Bradford was an inventor and brain trust, and best friends with Marlena Evans. He fell madly in love with dress designer Calliope Jones, whose trademark was her endless array of hats… which were very creative and outlandish to say the least! She later became a successful wedding planner. Eugene and Calliope's eccentric love story was a true original.

- **Reggie and Martha's Wedding Goes to the Dogs**—In a *Days of our Lives* first, the love of two pooches taking their vows was all the rage. Calliope Jones' dog, Martha, married dog Reggie Dubois! Accompanied by their wedding song, "How Much Is That Doggy in the Window," the nuptials were officiated by Robert LeClair. The "Father of the Bride," Dr. Neil Curtis, even walked Martha down the aisle. Despite a few hiccups, these dogs were pronounced doggy husband and wife!

- **"Take it off" for a good cause**—Dr. Cameron Davis was in serious debt and needed to make some extra money on the side. So the good doc took to stripping on the side! When University Hospital's Director of H.R. , Anne Milbauer, got wind of this, she headed to the club where he was baring all to get Cameron fired from the staff! But, thanks to Abigail Deveraux (who got wind of Anne's plans), she smartly gathered Brady, Rafe, and Daniel and got the men to strip, too… all in the name of a charity fundraiser. Abigail also gathered some of the Salem women to come to the club to "support the cause"! Even grandma Caroline Brady got an eyeful, and enjoyed donating a few bucks to help Cameron's cause!

- **CT (CAT) Scanner Revue Variety Show**—In an effort to raise money for a new CAT scan for University Hospital, the doctors, and family and friends put on a variety show benefit that dazzled all of Salem. In the revue Alice Horton did a sketch as Groucho Marx! Doug Williams sang and danced throughout, and Maggie Horton showed her dance prowess. Julie Williams, Donna and Don Craig, Robert LeClair, Dr. Tom Horton, Dr. Greg Peters, and Mickey Horton all participated in one unforgettable night!

JULIE REMEMBERS DOUG'S PLACE

"Originally, 'Doug's Place' was called 'Sergio's.' My mother, Addie, bought it for Doug as a wedding gift so that everyone in Salem could come and enjoy hearing his marvelous voice. It was there that my darling Doug sang many tender ballads to star-crossed lovers. The music always underscored our stories. Sometimes you'd hear an upbeat tune, sometimes it'd be the blues, but the songs would always reflect what people were thinking and feeling.

We had other wonderful singers join us over the years, including Trish Clayton (Patty Weaver) and her mother, Jeri Clayton (Kaye Stevens), and Liz Chandler (Gloria Loring). Robert LeClair (Robert Clary) sang solos and duets so many times! Eventually, 'Doug's Place' was closed, but we built a casino on the old Chisholm Mansion and opened up a new club—'Doug's Place on the Lake,' complete with a casino!

We discovered years later that there was literally a connection between 'Doug's Place on the Lake' and Stefano DiMera! It turns out there was a secret passageway that connected our new place to the DiMera Mansion. Doug and I faked a separation in order to get to the bottom of everything during which time I was romanced by the Phoenix himself!"

"After we left Salem to travel the world, Neil Curtis bought the place as a gift for Liz and renamed it 'Blondie's,' which was his nickname for her. After that, the club was renamed 'Wings,' but for my darling Doug and me, it will always be 'Doug's Place on the Lake.'

Much of the time we were in 'Doug's Place' and ' Doug's Place on the Lake,' Doug and I were not together. There was a lot of unrequited love. He'd sing a love song and I'd sit there and cry and somehow that played really well. It was at his club that he made the announcement that he'd married Lee Dumonde after I came back to Salem, having had surgery to heal the scars that I endured in the fire. Moments at 'Doug's Place' were always enriched and amplified by music. Most couples get one love song. I always like to think Doug's and my love was so strong we were blessed with two—'The Look of Love' and 'The Most Beautiful Girl.' He'd sing those songs to me and the audience would go crazy… and so would I!"

REGGIE AND MARTHA'S WEDDING

"And they called it puppy love…"

Days of our Lives has produced a lot of memorable weddings over 50 years, but the one broadcast on April 16, 1987 was for the dogs—literally! The writers combined the love fans have for their pooches with the show's trademark romantic marriage ceremonies when they wrote the episode in which Calliope's dog Martha wed Reggie DuBois!

Little Noelle Curtis acted as the flower girl. The pianist played "How Much Is That Doggie in the Window" as guests, including a very proud Calliope, made their way down the aisle. Neil Curtis aka "father of the bride" escorted Martha to the altar as the traditional bridal march was played. Martha wore a small veil; Eddie was looking dapper in his white hat and collar.

Robert LeClair officiated at the ceremony. Just as he asked if there was anyone present who objected to the two dogs getting married, Angelica Deveraux arrived and incredulously commented, upon seeing the canine ceremony, "You're kidding!"

Neil quickly silenced Angelica and Robert completed the ceremony! As the newlyweds were escorted away, Chris Kositchek quipped, "If I hadn't seen it, I wouldn't have believed it!"

NBC Photo

Press Department / 30 Rockefeller Plaza / New York. N.Y. 10020

IN CONCERT -- Grammy Award-winner Al Jarreau gave a benefit performance at NBC on April 11 of this year that will figure as part of the storyline of the daytime drama series "Days of Our Lives," in which he will make his acting debut, playing himself, Monday and Tuesday, April 30 and May 1 (1-2 p.m. NYT; Noon-I p.m. PT).   Joining him for a duet was Gloria Loring, who stars as Liz Chandler in the series. The Jarreau concert will figure in the series, Friday, May 4, and Monday-Tuesday, May 7-8. The actual concert before an audience at NBC, was a benefit for the Juvenile Diabetes Foundation. In the finale, Loring and Jarreau sang "Take Me to the Pilot" by Elton John.

(ABC) (SFP #1)   (4/20/84)

TAKING IT ALL OFF FOR CHARITY

Abigail and Chad learned Cameron was secretly stripping to earn money to repay a loan he had taken to help his mom, Celeste. Anne overheard Abigail and Chad talking about it and took the hospital administrator to the club to get Cameron fired. But Abigail caught wind of this, and so she got a bunch of guys (Brady, Rafe, and Daniel) to show up and strip too, claiming it was for a charity event.

"I'll never forget the variety show where all of us showed our talents to raise money for a new cat-scan for University Hospital. Maggie 'wowed' the audience with her dancing prowess, Grandma Alice literally became Groucho Marx before our eyes, and my husband Doug was a very busy man—appearing throughout the show. The talent was amazing. It was an unforgettable evening!"

Julie

REVIEW OF THE CT (CAT) SCANNER REVUE—Michael Maloney

Days of our Lives combined its unparalleled stable of singers with a story point that had University Hospital wanting a CT (CAT) Scanner in order to put on a memorable telethon (within the show) known as The CT Scanner Revue!

"It all started with the advent of the singers and songs at Doug's Place," says Bill Hayes, whose character Doug Williams was the owner/headliner at the nightclub. Very often, Hayes would perform songs on the show twice a week, but the singing wasn't done arbitrarily. "The songs were essential to the plots. The songs would be performances, of course, but the lyrics would reflect what characters like Neil or Don or Julie were thinking and feeling."

In 1979, Hayes brought the idea to utilize all the show's wonderful singers by putting on a show to producer Wes Kenney and head writer Ann Marcus, who greenlit the concept.

One of the most enthusiastic cast members of the variety show was Macdonald Carey (Tom). "He was thrilled," Hayes recalls. "He did an old number that Ray Bolger performed called 'The Old Soft Shoe.' And he did a wonderful job! The lyrics start off, 'When me and my Alice were playing the palace...' The look on Mac's face was wonderful!"

Hayes felt that it'd be a great idea to bring in seasoned choreographer/director Jack Bunch to stage the show. "Jack and I went through the script and added all the jokes," Hayes recalls. "Then we got a little bit more in the budget. Music director Jack Quigley did the arrangements, which classed up the show a bit more."

The CT Scanner Revue paid tribute to such Hollywood legends as The Marx Brothers, Shirley Temple, and many more!

"Ken Corday (son of *Days of our Lives* creator Ted Corday and then-executive producer Betty Corday) played the drums," says Susan Seaforth Hayes (Julie).

"Ken would throw the rubber chicken—which we had instead of a duck—and it would hit Jed Allan (aka Margaret Dumont) in the head," says Hayes. "It was wonderful! Suzanne Rogers (Maggie) did a tap dance to 'Get Happy!' Peter Brown (Greg) was used to being in cowboy shows, but, here, his face kept saying, 'I'm in a musical!'"

"It was good to look at his face because he missed every dance step," says Susan, lovingly. "He's the one guy in the line going to the right when everyone else is going to the left, but it didn't matter."

The numbers in the revue were lively, entertaining, nostalgic—not to mention racy! "I played the fiddle while Susan did a striptease," says Hayes.

"I took off a lot," Susan recalls. "I went down to a black lace bustier and black tights. The idea was the musician in the front, Bill, was playing a little ditty on his violin. It's not so great, but behind him is a girl stripping and he doesn't know it. I'd take off a little more each time. It was a comic striptease!"

Here's a partial list of *Days of our Lives* actors/characters from The CT Scanner Revue:

Macdonald Carey (Tom)—The Old Soft Shoe	Frances Reid (Alice)—Groucho
Bill Hayes (Doug)—Chico	Susan Seaforth Hayes (Julie)—Harpo
Jed Allan (Don)—Margaret Dumont	Peter Brown (Greg)—chorus
Suzanne Rogers (Maggie)—dancer	Mark Tapscott (Bob)—trumpet player
Robert Clary (Robert)—Shirley Temple	

BO AND HOPE'S ROMANTIC REUNION

After months of being held captive in Princess Gina's castle, Hope was rescued by Bo and brought back to Salem. To celebrate her homecoming, Bo decorated the *Fancy Face II*, where the couple shared a night of blissful romance. They made love for the first time in a very long time, and the next morning, Bo and Hope took their friend's boat out onto the water to watch the sunrise. It was the perfect way to put the traumatic events of the last year behind them and recommit their love for one another.

Days of our Lives has had many "firsts" throughout its 50 years on the air… tackling issues of the day head on, shedding light on under-represented segments of the population, and unexplored topics for the daytime landscape. From marriage equality, interracial romance, converting religions, medical crises, and diversity, *Days of our Lives* has handled each of these through powerful and effective storytelling, and moving performances, ensuring that they reflect the times we live in.

- 2014—Sonny Kiriakis and Will Horton said their vows, and their "I do's" in front of supportive family and friends, becoming the first gay male couple that are central characters to a soap opera to ever be married on the air.

- 1980—Marlena and her husband Don Craig welcomed into the world their beloved son, D.J. Only the baby died from Sudden Infant Death Syndrome (SIDS). *Days of our Lives* did not inform the audience of this story point ahead of time via spoilers wanting the audience to experience the shock just as Marlena would in this real-to-life devastating tragedy.

- 1986—Robin Jacobs, Chief of Surgery at University Hospital, fell in love with Dr. Mike Horton. Only Robin was a strict orthodox Jew, who was torn between her love for the good doc and her religion. After having a child with him after a one-night stand, then marrying into her own faith, she was unhappy, as she loved Mike. For the first time a Horton decided to begin converting to Judaism. However, Robin eventually left for Israel with their son, thinking they could never be happy.

- 1976—The Grant family became the first featured African American family on *Days of our Lives*, when David Banning took off in a car and went into the river and was believed to be dead. However, he stumbled out of the water and was taken in by the Grant family.

- 1976—David Banning fell in love with Valerie Grant, making it the first interracial romance on daytime soaps. The controversial relationship produced the first interracial kiss and first interracial engagement.

There was another type of groundbreaking first for *Days of our Lives* in 1976, and this one belonged to pop culture! At the height of their on-screen love story and popularity, Bill and Susan Seaforth Hayes became the first soap opera stars to appear on the cover of *TIME*, a major news magazine, as their characters Doug and Julie.

"At the time, *TIME* magazine photographed every soap on the air. They chose us for the cover!"
— Susan Seaforth Hayes

"An unparalleled penchant for creating unforgettable "supercouples" and groundbreaking story lines— like daytime's first interracial kiss and exorcism—has long set *Days of our Lives* apart from the rest of the soap opera world. It is the show with the most rabid fan base, whose devotion through thick and thin has played a huge part in its 50 years of success."
— Janet Di Lauro, Daytime Journalist

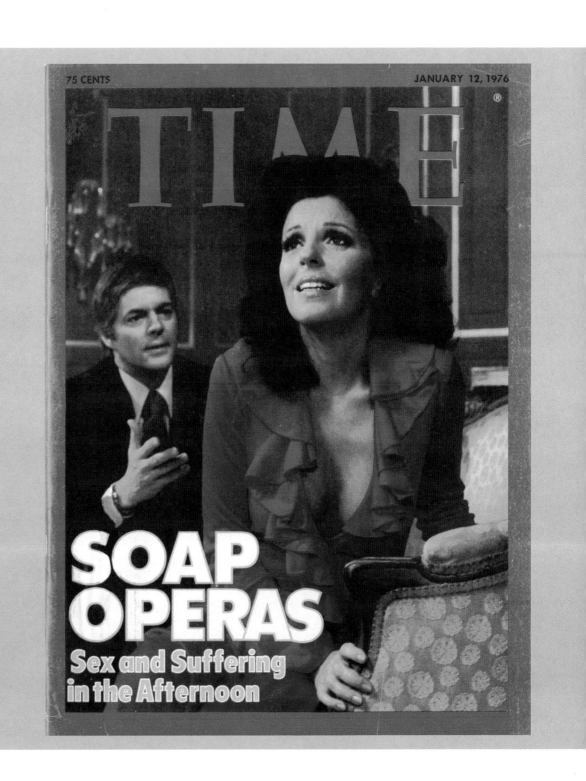

THE GRANT FAMILY

David Banning drove a car into the river and was believed to be dead. He stumbled out of the water and was taken care of by Paul and Helen Grant and their children, Valerie and Daniel—believed to be the first complete African American family on a daytime soap opera.

SAMI BRADY AND LUCAS HORTON'S "GREEN" WEDDING

Sami and Lucas were all set to have their happily-ever-after except for one small detail—Sami secretly feared she may be carrying EJ's child, not Lucas', after EJ had forced her to have sex with him. Hoping to create better luck for herself and Lucas, Sami suggested having a "green" wedding. There were many "green" elements to the wedding, which was held at St. Luke's (the reception was at Chez Rouge). They had soy candles to save energy. The clothes, invitations, and food were all organic. The food was provided by Ben Ford's restaurant, "Ford's Filling Station," while the silk dress was designed by Monique Lhuillier. The flowers were potted so they could be transplanted and reused after the ceremony. The party favors were handmade paper cards with seeds embedded in them—guests could plant the card to grow flowers.

Please take home
a seed packet.
Plant it ...
and watch the love grow.
Sami and Lucas

MARLENA AND DON'S BABY DIES OF SIDS

Newlyweds Don Craig and Dr. Marlena Evans were thrilled when they learned she was pregnant. After a rough pregnancy, Marlena gave birth prematurely to Don, Jr. A few months later, tragedy struck when a horrified Marlena found her son dead in his crib. D.J. had died of SIDS (Sudden Infant Death Syndrome). Don blamed Marlena for not taking better care of herself while she was pregnant. Although they tried to work things out, the strain on their marriage proved too much, and they finally divorced.

FIRST DAYTIME INTERRACIAL ROMANCE

When David was recuperating with the Grant family, he enjoyed being around a loving, warm environment—which was a stark contrast to his own upbringing. David and Valerie began to bond and eventually fell in love. David proposed, even though Valerie's parents worried about how difficult it might be for them as an interracial couple.

David ended up getting Trish Clayton pregnant from a one-night stand, and he and Valerie eventually broke up. Valerie headed to Washington, D.C. for medical school, while David married Trish, who gave brith to their son, Scotty.

THE WEDDING OF SONNY KIRIAKIS AND WILL HORTON

"May the love you share be a bond that brings you strength, comfort, and joy all the days of your lives."

— Marlena Evans

"I'm so relieved it's finally a world where we can truly know our precious boys. And they can be who they really are."

— Caroline Brady

EPISODE #12309

(C) KIRIAKIS MANSION W/EXTERIOR - DAY

(PICK UP AS CAROLINE GOES ON, STILL CLUTCHING
HER PRINTED TEXT, BUT NEVER OPENING THE PAGES.
IT'S UNCLEAR IF SHE EVEN REMEMBERS SHE'S
HOLDING HER SPEECH)

          CAROLINE

Robert could spin a yarn. He was Irish,
of course, more than a touch of the
blarney. And James could've finished
every sentence. You knew he'd heard 'em
all before, but he would laugh, that rat-
a-tat. Filled the whole pub.

(THE SILENT CONVERSATION CONTINUES BETWEEN THE
BRADYS, SHOULD SOMEBODY STEP IN?)

          CAROLINE (CONT'D)

So one day Robert comes in. Alone. He
sits at the bar and Shawn puts out their
usual. I'm about to ask "where's James"
when James comes in with this group of
people and sits at a table. Not a word
to Robert.

(SAMI, WHO WAS HALF OUT OF HER CHAIR TO GO GET
CAROLINE, NOW SITS BACK DOWN)

CAROLINE (CONT'D)

Like he didn't even know him. Sitting
with all these people calling him "Jimmy."
Nobody called him Jimmy, it was James.
Robert's at the bar and he doesn't even
turn around... just pours James's beer,
and then his own. And that beer sits.
And Robert sits there, looking at it.
Then it hits me like a shot. Those
people? It was James's family. Maybe
I'm slow but that's the first time I
knew for sure they were gay. I never
cared. But it never occurred to me what
it cost them either. I don't know which
one of them broke my heart more. In the
end, though, I knew who the real losers
were. That family. Because "Jimmy"
didn't laugh. He barely spoke. Their
own son, their brother... was a stranger
to them.

(A BEAT, THEN:)

CAROLINE (CONT'D)

When Will and his... Sonny first came to
me, I could tell they were nervous, but
all I could think was "hallelujah!" I'm
so relieved it's finally a world where
we can truly know our precious boys.
And they can be who they really are.
Congratulations, Sonny and Will. I wish
you a lifetime of laughter. And finishing
each other's sentences. If you live
long enough, some days that'll come in
real handy.

(AS CAROLINE KISSES BOTH BOYS ON THE CHEEK AND
HEADS BACK TO HER CHAIR, STILL CLUTCHING HER
UNOPENED SPEECH. [PRODUCTION: IF, IN THE
END, CAROLINE HAS READ THE SPEECH, AT THIS
POINT SHE'D START TO FOLD UP HER SPEECH AGAIN
AND WILL COULD REACH OUT A HAND FOR THE PAGES
AND TAKE IT FROM HER, MOVED, PUT IT INSIDE
HIS JACKET POCKET] ON REACTIONS)

FADE TO: BLACK

"Here we are, the Horton women having tea and donuts in Grandma Alice's living room—together—laughing, talking, crying… family supporting each other. Over the years many people have been served these tasty treats as they came seeking solace and guidance—a shoulder to lean on. Times change, but one thing is certain, in this house donuts will always be made with LOVE for the people who need that LOVE the most."

Love,
Julie

The Cordays—The Family Behind *Days of our Lives*

Executive Producer Ken Corday
Former Executive Producer Betty Corday
Co-Creator Ted Corday—not pictured.

Photo Credits

NBC/BNCU Photo Bank	**JPI Studios**
Gary Null, NBC	John Paschal/Celebrity Photo
Herb Ball, NBC	Howard Wise, JPI Studios
Chris Haston, NBC	Paul Skipper, JPI Studios
Paul Drinkwater, NBC	Jesse Grant, JPI Studios
Joseph Del Valle, NBC	Gerald Weinman, JPI Studios
Ron Tom, NBC	Aaron Montgomery, JPI Studios
Frank Carroll, NBC	Sean Smith, JPI Studios
Alice S. Hall, NBC	Jill Johnson, JPI Studios
Jean Krettler, NBC	Mike Guastella, JPI Studios
Mitchell Haaseth, NBC	Brian Lowe, JPI Studios
Jon Mckee, NBC	

Columbia Tristar Television International
Kathy Hutchins Photo Agency
Hutchins Photo Agency
Hutchins/Michelson Photography
Soap Opera Digest [Courtesy Of]
Jill Johnson Photography
Jeff Katz Photography
Tracey Morris Photography

Special thanks to special people

Elizabeth Gulick, Ryan Quan, Stephanie Sloane, Soap Opera Digest,
Susan Seaforth Hayes, Bill Hayes, Michael Fairman, Michael Maloney,
Suzanne Rogers, Deidre Hall, Maya Frangie, Dick Roberts,
Sherry Anderson Thomas, Scott Angelheart, NBC Photo Department,
Dena Higley, Ruby Montgomery, JPI Studios, Maureen Russell, Virginia King, Cindy
Irwin, Stephanie Bowen, Grace Menary-Winefield, Adrienne W. Krogh, and Tina Silva

Index

I so clearly remember that Monday, November 8,1965, being seven years old and home sick from school, sitting in the den with my mother. It was almost 2:00 p.m. (EST) and we were waiting for another show to come on. I reminded my mother that the new soap opera she had read about, *Days of our Lives*, starring MacDonald Carey was coming on. I read her the synopsis out of *TV Guide* and we decided to watch and give the new soap a chance. After that I watched it every day I was at home sick, or during a teacher work day, or holiday.

In 1966 I got a reel-to-reel tape recorder for Christmas and for my birthday in January,1967, I got a small black and white television. Using these and a G.E timer, I invented the first (so I believe) method of recording a television program for later "listening." I had everything precisely set so at 2 p.m. the timer turned on the television to NBC and *Days of our Lives*, and the reel-to-reel tape recorder, so that when I got home from school I could rewind the tape and listen to that day's episode!

Without becoming a "fanatic," over the years, many members of the cast of *Days of our Lives* became adopted family to me. As the unexpected only child of two parents in their midforties, I did not have many of the family members a normal person would have. Alice Horton, became the grandmother I never had, many of her children became my aunts and uncles... their children became my cousins... Men and women alike are drawn to the story lines and the characters in Salem. Watching so much of the medical content of the show helped me decide I wanted to pursue a career in the medical field. I entered college and obtained a degree as a clinical pharmacist.

Days of our Lives has enriched my life, brought me national fame in soap publications; has allowed me to forge friendships with Betty Corday, Frances Reid, Philece Sampler, Gregg Marx, Susan and Bill Hayes, Suzanne Rogers, Lauren Koslow, Drake Hogestyn, Camila Banus, Ken Corday, Greg Meng, and many others. I could never express my gratitude enough to Ken and Greg or CORDAY PRODUCTIONS for the many tangible and intangible things they have given me and done for me.

Unlike any other soap opera or television series, there is an indescribable bond between the show and its fans that will probably NEVER BE DEFINED. The series has brought me more pleasure than anything else in all the days of my life.

— Billy Vick, Rocky Mount, North Carolina,

    tagged by Ken Corday as *Days of our Lives* #1 fan.

Alice, Addie, Tom Jr., Marie, Tom, Bill, Laura, and Mickey